Training, productivity and labour competencies
in organisations

Leonard Mertens

Training, productivity and labour competencies in organisations

Concepts, Methodologies and Experiences

International Labour Office

CINTERFOR

MERTENS, L.
Training, productivity and labour competencies in organisations: concepts, methodologies and experiences. Montevideo : Cinterfor, 2004.
172 p. (Trazos de la Formación, 15)

Bibliografía: p. 169-172.
ISBN 92-9088-163-1
Título original: Formación, productividad y competencia laboral en las organizaciones: conceptos, metodologías y experiencias.

/FORMACIÓN/ /PRODUCTIVIDAD/ /COMPETENCIA/ /MEDICIÓN/ /EVALUACIÓN/ /METODOLOGÍA/ /AUTOINSTRUCCIÓN/ /INSTITUTO DE FORMACIÓN/ /EMPRESA/ /MÉXICO/ /REPÚBLICA DOMINICANA/ /PUB CINTERFOR/

ILO publications can be obtained through major booksellers or ILO local offices in many countries, or direct from ILO Publications, International Labour Office, CH 1211 Geneva 22, Switzerland. Catalogues or lists of new publications are available free of charge from the above address, or by e-mail to: pubvente@ilo.org. Web site: www.ilo.org/publns

The Inter-American Research and Documentation Centre on Vocational Training (Cinterfor/ILO) is an ILO technical service, set up in 1964 with the aim of encouraging and coordinating the action of the Latin American and Caribbean institutes, organisations and agencies involved in vocational training.

The Centre publications can be obtained through ILO local offices in many countries, or direct from Cinterfor/ILO, Casilla de correo 1761, e-mail: dirmvd@cinterfor.org.uy. Fax 902 1305, Montevideo, Uruguay

Web site: www.cinterfor.org.uy

Printed in Uruguay

CONTENTS

FOREWORD

Training has many manifestations and different purposes in the life of individuals and society. This document will look into one such manifestation, namely the links of training with the productivity and working conditions of organisations.

In its most elementary form, productivity is defined as the relationship between input and output. Improving that ratio would theoretically result in higher levels of welfare. This assumption is debatable for a number of reasons, in particular because country or enterprise statistics do not take into account all possible inputs. They specifically disregard those with no market price but undeniable social value, like for example noxious effects on the environment, deterioration of working conditions, physical and mental fatigue of workers, stress, and others. The same can be said of products or outputs which are not all necessarily socially useful and may even destroy social and natural assets (e.g the environment) as a result of which productivity would be negative for many countries and companies if such variables were to be considered (ILO, 2000).

In view of these measuring difficulties, not just any improvement in the productivity of organisations/enterprises is socially desirable, but only those stemming from a socially responsible management. If it fulfils this condition, productivity becomes the basis for welfare. It is in this sense that we use the term productivity in this paper.

Identifying the factors that determine an enhancement of productivity in organisations has been object of study by many analysts in the last century; some of them have emphasised theoretical aspects, others empirical ones. Inaddition they have also looked into the impact and effects of training initiatives on productivity.

There is plenty of normative literature on productivity and training management, addressed to managers and directors of organisations or to those that implement training programmes.

Less abundant are the studies interconnecting both aspects, explaining the conceptual framework underlying their own research and that of others, and suggesting a standard for a model or proposal that has been tried out and verified. This has been the aim of the present paper, according to the sequence recommended by authors like Deming for strategies to improve organisations: the rationale or conceptual framework should precede techniques or instruments (ILO, 2000).

The fundamental proposal of our work is to show that it is feasible and profitable to improve the productivity and working conditions by promoting the ongoing learning of the employed personnel. The notion itself is not new; what is new is the context in which the proposal is made, the direction given to training and the concrete and proven instruments used to implement it.

The relationship between training and productivity is viewed with the current backdrop of organisations, characterised by constant change, where information circulates with increasing ease and fluency, which requires the building and refashioning of new environments and methods for learning. Having formerly been mainly in the hands of educators, training is nowadays a strategic element analysed at board meetings of leading companies in the world. Attaining the best possible influence on the organisations' capacity to learn is the current challenge of directors and managers, as well as that of trade unionists that try to participate and guide the process of modernisation.

Traditional behaviourist training, with its structured and rigid curricula focusing on programmed teaching and deriving from a static view of the knowledge required by work processes, loses significance in this context (Román Diez, 1999). The fact is acknowledged that organisations learn in many different ways through the persons that make them up. Formal courses in classrooms are only one way (perhaps the least important one) in which organisations learn.

How can we bring influence to bear upon this complex and also very strategic process for organisations? If flexibility is one of the characteristics distinguishing modern organisations from their predecessors, would not the manner of influencing learning have to be flexible as well? Flexible in the use of teaching techniques and the structuring of contents, in the time and place of instruction, with open access and in accordance with specific needs, these appear to be the new doctrines of training organisations (Haghey, 2000).

Flexible learning means that the traditional dividing line between those who teach and those who learn vanishes, the split between operation and training, between theory and practice, the needs of the organisation and those of the individual, explanation and evaluation, explicit and tacit knowledge, costs and benefits. Having lost its traditional mantle, training management calls for new processes and instruments.

Flexibility, adaptability, fitting into context and above all focusing on learning rather than on teaching, are some of the characteristics that training processes and instruments have to comply. The risk implicit in opening up training spaces is loss of control, as the process becomes more complex. Focalisation on the one hand, and striving for improved productivity and working conditions on the other, seem to be the main guidelines of training management for organisations.

This paper approaches training from the overall angle of organisations, not just as an isolated effort to train individuals. It is interrelated with the management of knowledge and training organisations, where the concept of learning is made extensive to the organisation as a whole.

It specifically analyses training management forms and instruments, making it possible to modify the enhancement of productivity and working conditions in firms and enterprises in Latin America. To that end it cites concrete experiences of methodologies tried out in companies of countries of the region, mainly Mexico and the Dominican Republic.

Preparation of the paper was possible thanks to the collaboration of the ILO InFocus Programme on Skills, Knowledge and Employability and to the increasing co-operation and joint work of Cinterfor/ILO and that Programme.

1
CONCEPTUAL FRAMEWORK: APPROXIMATION TO A MODEL

Organisations often have a static view of the relationship between training and productivity, especially when they consider their operational personnel. This view is normally there in an implicit manner and does not respond to a strategic plan. It works unconsciously and evolves as it goes along, routinely.

It would be wrong to suggest that this static view is dysfunctional for organisations. It plays an important role, particularly in the incorporation of newly recruited personnel. It is also functional for keeping existing personnel updated in their knowledge and skills. Getting operatives to comply with the procedures deriving from the technical design of their productive process is in itself an achievement for many organisations, considering their current situation. The absence of clear-cut and/or updated procedures appears to be the rule rather than the exception in Latin American organisations. Systematic initiatives to train operational personnel in prescribed procedures is seldom part of their everyday practice.

In the present day context of rapid and unpredictable changes in market places, technologies and institutional frameworks, in which information is increasingly easier to obtain, a static view of the training/productivity relationship is necessarily limited. Faced with such limitation and the negligible development of conceptual structures capable of analysing that correlation dynamically, we shall put forward another proposal that for many years has been at the root of concrete applications by various organisations of the region.

a. Static approach: training/productivity

The training approach that has traditionally prevailed in organisations –especially for production workers– aims at teaching them how to perform the tasks of their respective work posts. By complying with task descriptions as documented and/or handed down by colleagues, workers will then be doing what the organisation expects of them, in the way of productivity.

This has not always been easily put into practice. Reality has been more complex than the tasks described or the know-how passed on by fellow workers. Its foundations are to be found not only in Taylor's notions on the scientific management of work, at the beginning of the century, but on Schumpeter's theories, who was one of the most important theorists of modern capitalism. He established a link between innovation in microeconomics and macroeconomic development. For Schumpeter, the creativity and leadership of an entrepreneur are the source of innovation and productivity. Entrepreneurs can normally play this role during a certain period of their lives: "...they are only entrepreneurs when they effectively put new arrangements into practice, and lose that character when their business has been set in motion".

According to him, entrepreneurial leadership "...leads means of production along new paths. However, the employer does not do so by persuading men to implement his plans (...) but by buying them or their services to do as he sees fit" (Schumpeter, 1997). In this *schumpeterean* picture, operational personnel was envisaged as a passive rather than active subject in the process of innovation, which was in keeping with the entrepreneurial practices of the times.

Nowadays many organisations still adhere, implicitly or explicitly, to this principle in their training strategies for operational personnel. For the less developed segment of enterprises in Latin America –which generally lack uniform criteria for the performance of tasks and functions- the "mere" fact that personnel are trained in the correct performance of tasks in "normal" operational circumstances and according to parameters derived from a detailed analysis of the process involved, may represent a significant improvement of productivity.[1] In this way organisations may tap productivity reserves through training and according to the dictates of their technical management.

Figure 1 shows this in a simplified manner. There is a given value of technical labour productivity for each competency (qualification) required of personnel members, that only varies in time when technical or organisational changes are introduced. Raising labour productivity from its level at moment (t1) to that of moment (t2) means tapping the static labour productivity reserve existing in the organisation. How is this done? By deepening and broadening each one of

---

1   The occurrence of changes in economic structures does not necessary mean that "old" methods for raising productivity have died out. They continue to be valid, specially in economically less sophisticated countries (ILO, 2000).

the competencies (qualifications) of the employed personnel according to previously defined standards, derived from the technical parameters of the process involved.

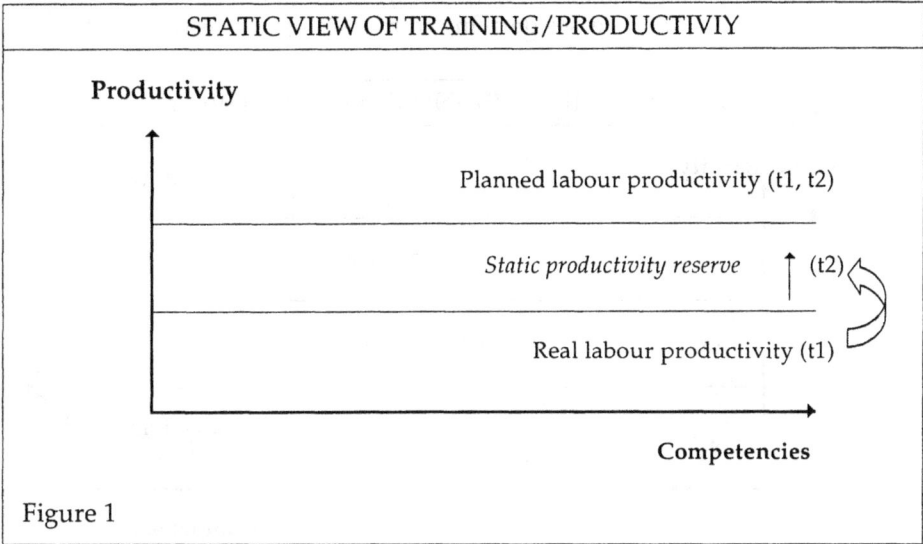

STATIC VIEW OF TRAINING/PRODUCTIVIY

Productivity

Planned labour productivity (t1, t2)

Static productivity reserve   ↑ (t2)

Real labour productivity (t1)

Competencies

Figure 1

However, the current context of organisational dynamics and the relationship between training and productivity have a specific significance that goes beyond the technical description of the process in static and planned operational conditions. As a result of the globalisation of markets and the characteristics of new technologies the training/productivity equation acquires a more dynamic and less predictable dimension. The hypothesis has been put forward that the future of many leading (and non-leading) organisations of the region in their respective markets will to a good extent depend on their capacity to venture into the new relationship between training and productivity that is described below.

b.   Dynamic approach: training/productivity

The dynamic approach to the relationship between training and productivity stems from the general and schematic principle that productivity enhancement is the basis for entrepreneurial competitiveness, for a country's competitive capacity and the welfare of its population. If we accept that productivity enhancement is the result of innovation, defined as the successful application of new knowledge to organisations, we have established its dynamic/interactive relationship with training and occupational competencies (learning).[2]

In this perspective, developing competencies in workers leads to an increase of the technically desired labour productivity, through innovation and the constant improvement of processes deriving from training efforts (Figure 2).

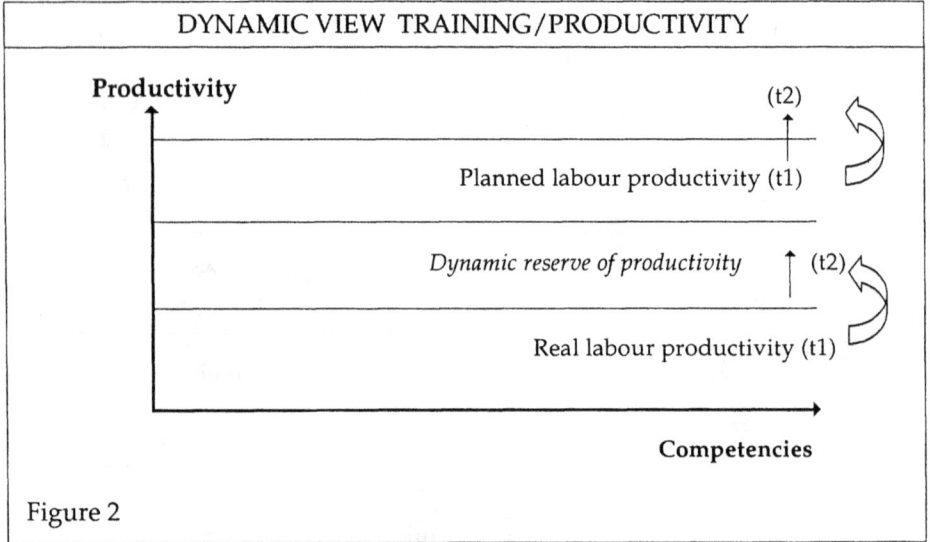

DYNAMIC VIEW TRAINING/PRODUCTIVITY

Productivity

(t2)

Planned labour productivity (t1)

Dynamic reserve of productivity (t2)

Real labour productivity (t1)

Competencies

Figure 2

As raised productivity allows for -and also requires- improving the working conditions under which it is generated, we have established a conceptual and dynamic relationship between improved productivity and training and decent work[3] (ILO, 2001).

> *"The literature of organisational culture has not yet managed to keep its promise of explaining soundly how to create organisations that are pleasant to work in, passionate for their personnel and yield a profit"* (Galunic ; Weeks 2001).

---

2   Training is not the only determining factor in the application of new knowledge in organisations. Another source is new equipment that brings along fresh knowledge.

3   The meaning and purpose of the term 'decent work' cannot be conveyed in a single phrase or definition. It comprises the employment and future prospects of workers; their working conditions; the balance of work and family life; the schooling of children and avoidance of child labour; gender equity, egalitarian recognition of men and women; personal abilities to compete in labour markets, keeping updated in the skills of new technologies, and in health preservation; participation at the workplace, letting the voice of workers be heard; it is the path from survival to existence, ensuring human dignity (ILO, 2001).

The mutually reinforcing nature of the various aspects that make up the notion of decent work, and the fact that it is an eminently systemic concept, has been emphasised in most of the literature on decent work. In that sense, regarding the link between training and productivity (both of them essential components of decent work), we may conclude that "there is basic consensus that it is not possible to introduce or use efficiently any new technique or modern plan for that purpose (enhancing productivity) without well trained and properly instructed personnel at all levels of a country's economy".[4]

This model describes how concepts are interlinked. It is a form of visualising and representing organisations through a breakdown of the organisational learning process, which in practice is seen as a whole.

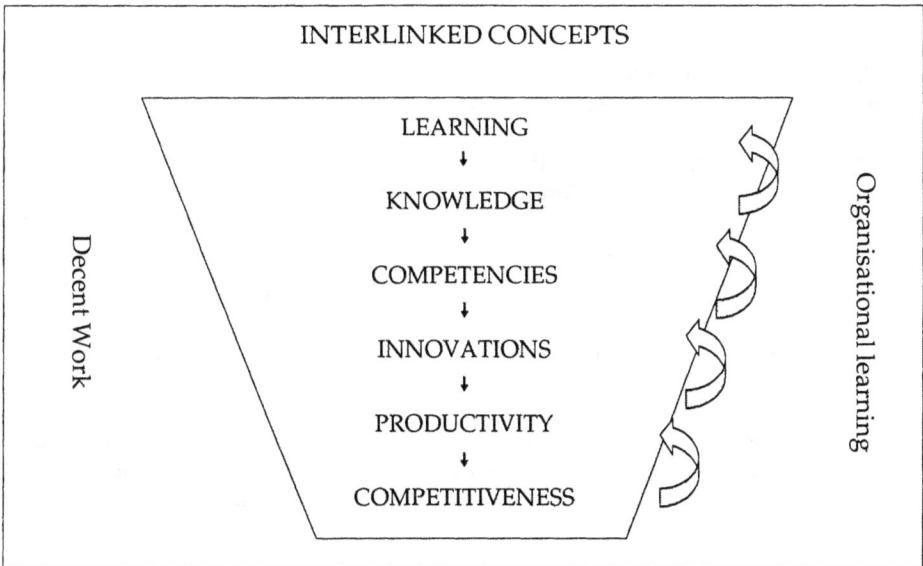

INTERLINKED CONCEPTS

LEARNING
↓
KNOWLEDGE
↓
COMPETENCIES
↓
INNOVATIONS
↓
PRODUCTIVITY
↓
COMPETITIVENESS

Decent Work

Organisational learning

The breakdown of the model as analysed below enables us to identify the incidents ocurring most frequently in each link of the chain. This clarifies on which aspects organisations must focus when they invest in personnel development to promote the generation and application of new knowledge.

| 4   Cinterfor/ILO: Training for decent work; Montevideo, Cinterfor, 2001.

Learning

Learning is the basis of the link between training and the productivity of organisations. The theory is that in order to have an effect on productivity, organisations should concentrate on how to learn rather than what to learn. "Learning can only be improved when we think on how we do it" (Román Diez, 1999).

Learning is rather a vague concept, as it is used in various contexts with different meanings. It refers both to processes and to results. "Learning is a process that modifies the stock of knowledge of an individual or organisation" (Sánchez; Heene 2000).

This process can take place in two stages: a primary moment and a target stage. The first one leads to new knowledge. The target stage leads to grasping how to improve the process of knowledge generation that results in higher productivity and competitiveness for organisations. It can be termed 'organisational learning' aimed at learning to learn.

It would be naïve to think that learning processes in organisations will be harmonious and linear. In organisations the dilemmas, conflicts, inconsistencies and special interests of individuals and groups are part of learning processes (ibidem). Management instruments and procedures intended to influence organisational learning will have to face the challenge of adequately dealing with the social factors that may emerge.[5] It is not unusual to see innovative and well designed productivity-related training proposals go down due to mishandling of social and power relations within organisations.

Application of the methodologies presented in this document has successfully passed those contingency aspects that in each organisation manifest themselves differently. It can be held that such contingency factors shape up the path of organisational learning (ibidem).

---

5   The significance of influencing organisational culture – including management, power and policy –cannot be overemphasised in the application of learning. In this manner, learning is invested with a technical dimension, as well as a political and cultural one (Jakupec; Garrick, 2000).

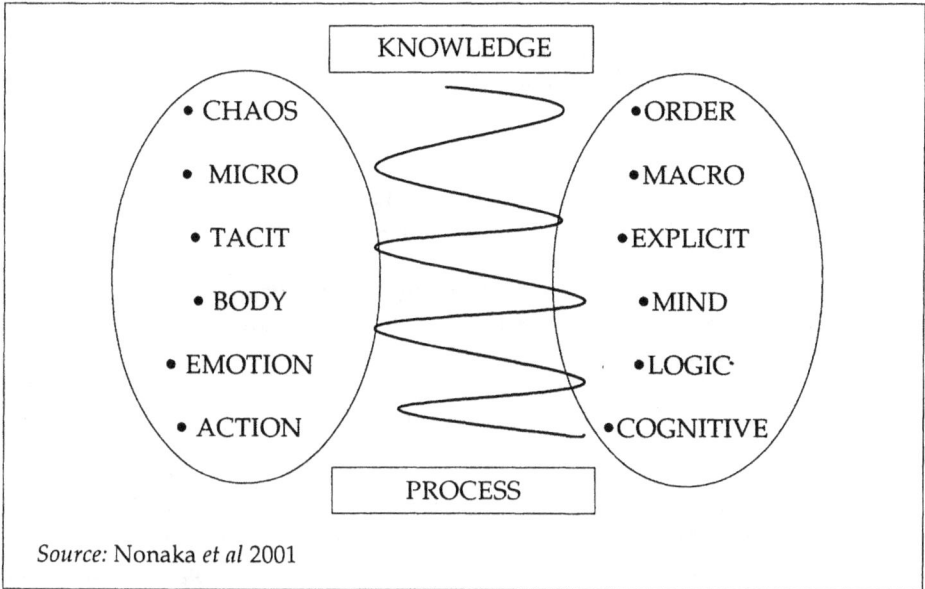

KNOWLEDGE

- CHAOS
- MICRO
- TACIT
- BODY
- EMOTION
- ACTION

- ORDER
- MACRO
- EXPLICIT
- MIND
- LOGIC·
- COGNITIVE

PROCESS

Source: Nonaka *et al* 2001

It follows from the above that organisations must focus on the process of "learning to learn" in introducing these methodologies. It is the most intensive and energy-consuming stage of the whole process of development and application.

Knowledge

In accordance with the conceptual model, learning from experience and/or study generates new knowledge in organisations. This is the first screening or selection mechanism: not all learning processes lead to new knowledge. In the viewpoint of organisations, it is necessary to lay stress on that screening to ensure that learning efforts are not in vain.

Knowledge is a broad notion that includes depth in understanding phenomena, interpretation and information. It is distinguished from information by the inclusion of interpretation, beliefs and a higher level of validity. Organisational knowledge refers to the sum of knowledge and information that organisations have and share in full or in part; it is normally stored in operational procedures, routines and regulations. In a pragmatic perspective we can say that organisational knowledge emerges through learning in experiences of problem solving (Schultz, 2001).

> ...*knowledge cannot be managed... only the technological, organisational and social environment can be managed that causes knowledge to be shared and recreated...*

A social dimension is also included in the concept of knowledge we have adopted here: a justified and true belief (Nonaka *et al*, 2001).

Knowledge is dynamic and it is created in the social interaction between individuals and organisations. It is specific to a context: devoid of that context it is just information, not knowledge. It is humanistic because it pertains to the behaviour of men. With these appurtenances, knowledge can be defined as a dynamic and humanistic process justifying personal belief towards the 'truth' (ibidem).

Knowledge may be tacit or tangible: the knowledge based on subjective points of view, intuitions or perceptions versus coded knowledge expressed in a formal and systematic language, that can be shared in the form of data, formulae, specifications and manuals. Learning instruments will have to point in the direction of these two spheres of knowledge in order to influence the productivity or organisations. This should be the thrust of knowledge management.

Knowledge management can be defined as "the way in which organisations obtain, share out and gain commercial advantages from their intellectual capital", and intellectual capital would be "the value of the knowledge and experience of the organisations' labour force and their accumulated memory" (Warner, 2001).

The paradox of this definition is that knowledge is not managed directly because it is part of persons, their intellectual capital. It is managed indirectly through social, organisational and technical mechanisms that enable knowledge to be shared and recreated.

Technical aspects taken from practice have to be generated, and inversely, theoretical aspects have to be introduced into practice. It is not just an exchange between practice and theory; it also implies acting on the learners' subjectivity in coordination with the targeted knowledge. "Knowledge is mainly generated through the interaction of tacit and explicit knowledge, and to a much lesser degree only from tacit or explicit knowledge" (ibidem).

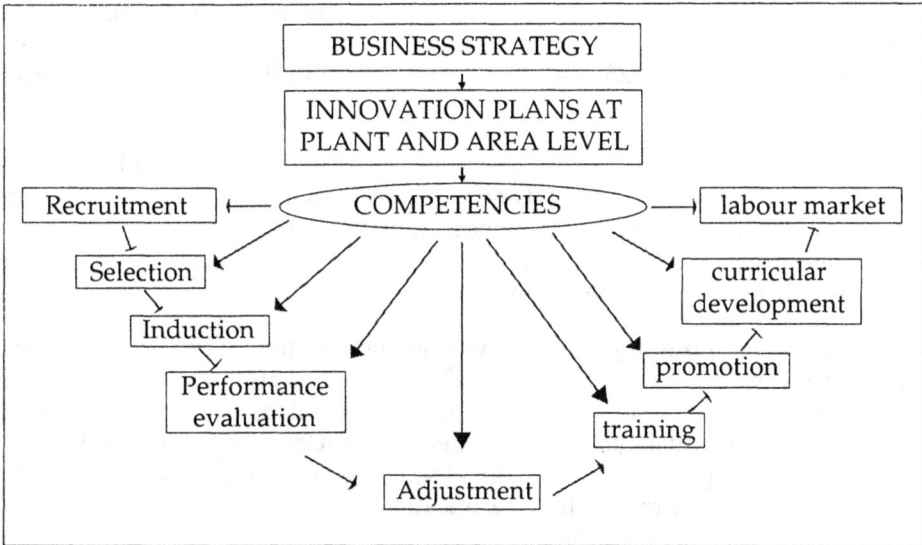

Competencies

The following "link" are the competencies or qualifications, i.e. the capabilities shown by workers or the results of the knowledge they have put into practice at organisational and individual levels. It is not the summation of all their abilities but only of those that reflect the organisation's objectives in the performance of each one of its collaborators. It is again a screen and a selection process. Not all knowledge leads to the desired and/or expected results, and very little of it makes the organisation stand out or be exceptional. There is a risk that organisational memory may be neglected and that some know-how be lost.

Competencies are an important stage in the organisational learning process because they can be managed and acted upon directly. Neither learning nor knowledge can be managed in a direct way: they are intrinsic processes in individuals and organisations. But competencies can be handled directly and from there we can measure the organisational learning process and secure organisational memory as well. In general, the assessment of competencies is fundamentally qualitative, whereas productivity – just in terms of efficiency- is normally measured in a quantitative manner. Competencies are a complex phenomenon, in which a person's performance is evaluated in relation to previously formulated expectations, but also according to certain perceptions of client satisfaction and other positive intangibles results (Del Bueno, 2001).

At organisational level, competencies contribute to the development of an organisational memory, i.e. internal structures that store up knowledge in one way or another, like databases, work procedures and the architecture of products and services.

Organisations learn because they have infrastructures that go beyond the cognitive process of an individual and expanded social networks. The important thing is that in organisations knowledge is translated into processes, reports' structures, performance management and processes for the comparison of resources that provide guidance for company directors.

In the field of training, competencies are not limited to the training process in the strict sense of the word. They make it possible to attune all the subsystems of personnel (human resources) management to global results, without divesting them of their individual dynamics and internal characteristics. Competencies unify and focalise sub-processes of personnel selection, training, evaluation and careers plans, as well as recognition (certification), so as to reinforce each other and enhance organisational learning.

There are different views of competencies, as there are of knowledge and learning. The one we have adopted here is that building capabilities by means of competencies has its own pragmatism. In present-day contexts it implies teaching individuals to think and act in the world. Personnel in general and workers in particular must not only rethink their tasks and functions, but think about themselves. They have to develop a capacity for responding to unforeseen market situations at any moment. "They have to turn from passive into active subjects, working with and against the strains of new workplaces". (Garrick, 2000).

To instil in persons this capacity for thinking, competencies should not only guide them in the tasks and functions that markets require in "normal" or planned situations, but must endow them with "surplus" knowledge and understanding enabling them to act appropriately in changing situations. Establishing that "surplus" will depend on organisational vision and culture. However, in current contexts it is considered a "not negotiable" extra that persons in an organisation must comprehend how they contribute to generating the value of that organisation, who its clients are and the factors for their satisfaction, and with whom they must maintain horizontal as well as vertical communication.

Competencies also make it possible to include aspects for enhancing the quality of employment, such as safety and health, communication, values and attitudes. The development of competency profiles and self-training as an important component of learning imply the participation of the workers involved in the design and application of instruments. Coverage of such fields –stemming from competencies' management– will in the last resort depend on the organisational culture.

> *"Keeping personnel focused on what they know well is a good way of reproducing the ideas an organisation already has, but a bad way of promoting innovation* (Galunik; Weeks, 2001).

Innovations

Innovations can be defined as the application of new knowledge and/or new interpretations and permutations of existing knowledge to productive processes (Johnson, 1992). Competencies express knowledge put into practice, which does not necessarily mean the application of new knowledge. Here we come to another screen or selection mechanisms in the chain of learning.

The process of innovation implies a moment of "creative destruction of knowledge" and existing competencies, specially in the case of radical changes (Langlois; Robertson, 1995). This does not mean breaking up with all the organisational memory but only with some of its aspects. Organisations are faced with the alternative of exploiting existing routines or exploring new ones (Cohendet; Lerna, 1997).

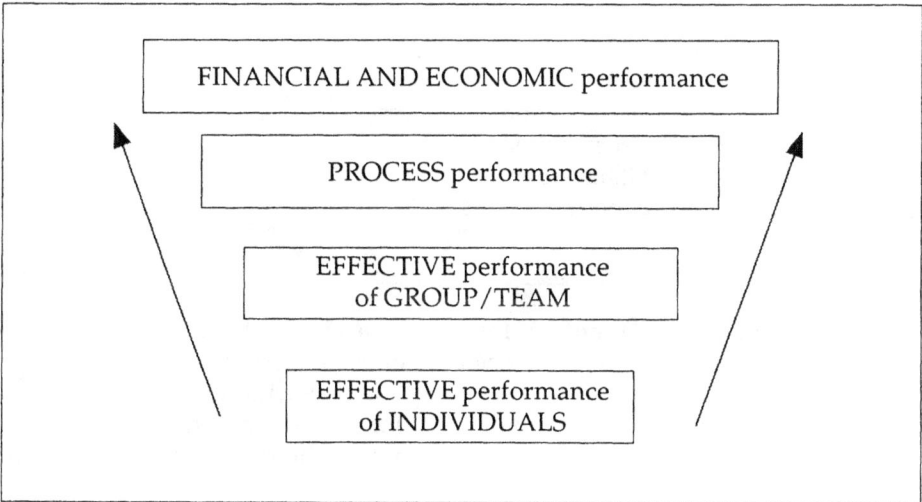

The important point here is that an effort is made to break up with the accepted idea that learning processes are generally very conservative and tend to reinforce existing frames of reference, continuing with existing knowledge. Much more difficult and less accepted by organisations is the strategy of reaching a qualitatively higher level of knowledge and going beyond what already exists. Part of the strategy consists of motivating the personnel to move in the direction of this transcendental learning (Weggeman, 1997).

Competencies frequently refer to the organisational memory and are not always an instrument for innovation. Some authors have characterised competencies as intrinsically conservative and bound within existing limits.

Work, learning and innovation have traditionally been considered conflicting activities. Work practices and routines have been deemed conservative and resistant to change. Learning has been visualised apart form work and with difficulties for change. Innovation has been envisaged as a necessary imposition of change that interrupts work and learning routines. Interconnecting these three activities and making them mutually complementary requires recognising the importance of practice (Brown; Duguid, 2000).

IMPROVEMENT OF PRODUCTIVITY

$\triangle$ Productivity =

F (Innovation)

- Technology
- Organisation of processes (client oriented)
- Organisation of work
- Management of human resources
- Labour relations

The traditional divergence of these activities is due to abstract representations of practices and even to the negation of current practices. Correcting this requires a modification of work and the way competencies are defined, as well as learning forms, which are often confined to formal descriptions. If conceived as learning communities, organisations can shorten the distances between work (competencies), learning and innovation (ibidem).

For innovations to be translated into effective productivity improvements in organisations, innovative initiatives should not be limited to just one sphere. Empirical studies have shown that "...in order to achieve good performance, large organisations have to be good in many of their small subsystems" (Marsh 2001; Mertens 1997). Innovations must occur simultaneously in the areas of technology, the organisation of processes (specially client orientation), the organisation of work, the different subsystems of human resources' management and labour relations. From the point of view of innovation management, this means in practice than when launching a project or initiative in any one of these areas, coordination with all the others will be required to obtain an overall impact on the organisation.

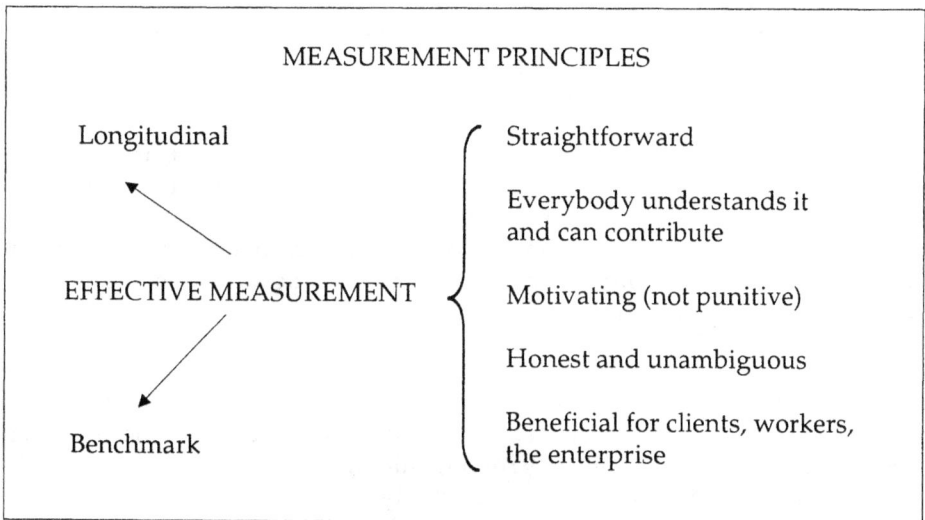

MEASUREMENT PRINCIPLES

Longitudinal

EFFECTIVE MEASUREMENT

Benchmark

Straightforward

Everybody understands it and can contribute

Motivating (not punitive)

Honest and unambiguous

Beneficial for clients, workers, the enterprise

> **Point of view 1:**
> *"Measurement leads to change. It may well begin with audits and then proceed to more complex programmes"*
> ILO/ Productivity Forum, 2001.

Productivity

Productivity improvements are the result of innovations added to the maintenance of successful existing practices. Here there are also screens and selection. Not all innovations necessarily lead to an improvement of overall productivity: there may be innovations in products and processes that improve one aspect but overlook others. For example, a new and innovative design can turn out to be too costly when producing it, or some innovation in the productive process may limit the possibility of introducing new product designs.

Productivity is nearly synonymous with measurement. It is measurement implying an assessment of organisational and individual learning, as it relates results to inputs. It is the point in the learning chain where measurement is most evident. There is a well known saying according to which the mere fact of beginning to measure raises productivity. Measurement encourages learning, which in turn enhances productivity.

It is important to emphasise this point because it explains a fundamental difference between the two methodologies for linking training/learning with productivity. The measurement of productivity can encourage and promote training and learning. Or the other way round, training and learning efforts are evaluated and guided by the results of productivity measurement.

> *"Traditional instruments for measuring productivity, like labour or capital productivity, expressed in terms of output per man hour, space, speed, etc. do not convey the essence of productivity ratios. Larger consistent frameworks are required".*
> ILO/ Productivity Forum, 2001.

Point of view 2:
*"The sole measurement of productivity does not promote changes in manage-
ment. Change itself has to be managed to complement measurement and turn
organisations into learning organisations".*
ILO/ Productivity Forum, 2001.

Measurement need not be restricted to quality and efficiency aspects but
may also include the concept of socially responsible productivity, or sustainable
productivity (ILO, 2001).

The increasing complexity of objectives that organisations pursue leads them
to go from partial to general instruments in their search for a systemic approach
for managing essential activities to improve productivity. This overall approach
in turn breaks down into subsystems, each one with its respective degree of complexity and specificity. One breakdown proposal could be: individual or group
activities, based on processes or on a global view (economic and financial, central
objectives).

The problem is the following: to have a global effect on organisations, a train-
ing/learning effort at the level of individuals would have to be coordinated with
changes or adaptations at subsequent levels (groups, processes). By contrast, if
organisations introduce modifications entailing learning and knowledge at the
level of processes, their impact on economic and financial aspects and on central
objectives is more immediate (Mertens, 1997).

Point of view 3:
*Measurement is the second stage after awareness. There are sophisticated mea-
surement systems and others evolved through teamwork; the latter have the
advantage that people believe in something that they themselves have built.
When it is integrated into the management of an organisation, measurement
leads to change and learning. Objectives have to be defined and measured, a
systematic improvement system has to be devised and a logical remuneration
system put in place".*
ILO/Productivity Forum, 2001.

That is the reason why most organisations centre on learning based on the
introduction of new processes. They are less inclined to go up the ladder from
"down below". Nevertheless, in view of changes in the work environment and

technological trends, some organisations are adopting the "long route" that starts with learning dynamics at individual level and subsequent collective coordination to achieve a significant impact on results and general objectives.

Employees generally associate the concept of productivity with costs reduction, starting by personnel cutbacks and increased workloads. This is indeed a real problem that has its impact and effects on the organisations' learning culture. When enterprises have laid stress on drastic costs reductions, the long route may be rather complicated. However, "productivity focalised exclusively on bringing down costs is possible and viable for a short while, but difficult to maintain in the long run. It would seem that client satisfaction has a different emphasis than just cutting costs, at least in the perspective of employment quality" (ILO/Productivity Forum, 2001). Insofar as this implies a change in the organisational culture it will cause resistance, in some cases based on short-term strategic views: "there is a tension between short-term views to get direct and immediate results *versus* change of culture instruments with a delayed effect" (ibidem).

Competitiveness

Competitiveness appears as the penultimate link in the learning chain. Its meaning differs for profit-making market organisations and non-profit ones. In both cases, however, regardless of their nature, they have elements in common that refer to client satisfaction: opportunity price; quality of products and processes; design and timeliness (flexibility, response capacity) of the goods or services offered. "Competitiveness is the ability always to secure the most advantageous position or niche in rapidly changing markets. The main determinant of this capacity to sell goods and services in the international market is no longer just the edge of relative costs. Competitiveness is increasingly based on quality, speed of response, technological superiority, product or service differentiation (Tolentino, 2000).

The screen and moment of selection is that improved productivity does not necessarily mean an improvement of competitive positioning in the market, or the achievement of proposed general objectives. Productivity is an intermediate expression between a result and an input. We have to establish if the result is accepted by the market and perceived as an improvement by customers.[6] Productivity is not synonymous with competitiveness, although the latter may re-

---

6   In the case of the sugar industry, that has to compete with high corn fructose, customers are looking not only for price but for food health, since high fructose has the advantage that its process is cleaner than that of cane sugar.

quire the former:[7] "the underlying determinant of competitiveness –either at national, sectoral or entrepreneurial level- is an increase in overall productivity blending the notion of efficiency with effectiveness" (ibidem).

Competitiveness is basically connected with the organisational ability of constantly creating added value for its customers. This in turn depends on the creativity of individuals and the support that the organisation of work can offer them for interacting and learning. When creativeness is the main determining factor of competitiveness, the relationship between an organisation's social capital and its productivity is almost self-explanatory. However, it is not sufficient to maintain or raise levels of capability or knowledge to enhance this kind of productivity. It is a necessary ingredient, but by itself it will not result in creativity or added value for customers. What this type of sustained productivity requires is something mysterious, intrinsic in the organisation itself and not easily definable[8] (ILO/Productivity Forum, 2001).

From the viewpoint of business management, one main concern is to develop future competitive advantages. The absence of a strategic approach might lead to learning processes following current standards and methods, which would entail non-optimal capabilities. Once the fields of knowledge that are critical for competitive success have been identified, appropriate learning strategies can be formulated that may be developed internally or externally – mergers, alliances, consultancies – (Cross; Israelit, 2000).

Organisational Learning and Quality of Employment (Decent Work)

The last link in the learning chain, that is also the end and the beginning of an imaginary cycle in the constantly moving process between learning/training and productivity competitiveness, is feedback, both regarding the effectiveness of learning in market terms and in improving conditions for decent work.

This is the process of "learning to learn" in the organisation, which is a learning process at another ontological level: meta-learning. One of the basic principles of meta-learning is that policies and programmes to improve productivity/competitiveness should be applied in a systematic manner.

---

7   It is worth noting that the competitiveness of enterprises may depend on factors other than productivity, such as an oligopolistic position or "natural" competitive advantages.

8   For instance, knowing to do what the competition cannot do, a capacity to innovate more rapidly than competitors, a suitable work environment, a company's entrepreneurship, its trademark or image, its quality as perceived by the public, customer loyalty, flexibility to adapt to drastic changes, etc.

Employment quality is generally measured by each one of the subsystems of human resources' development. The improvement of an indicator is frequently conditioned by the improvement of another one. It is advisable to handle indicators in the different subsystems to ensure their mutual support in the management of human development.

Interaction that
must be ensured

training

job stability

ergonomics,
work conditions

participation   remuneration

Human resources' development
subsystems

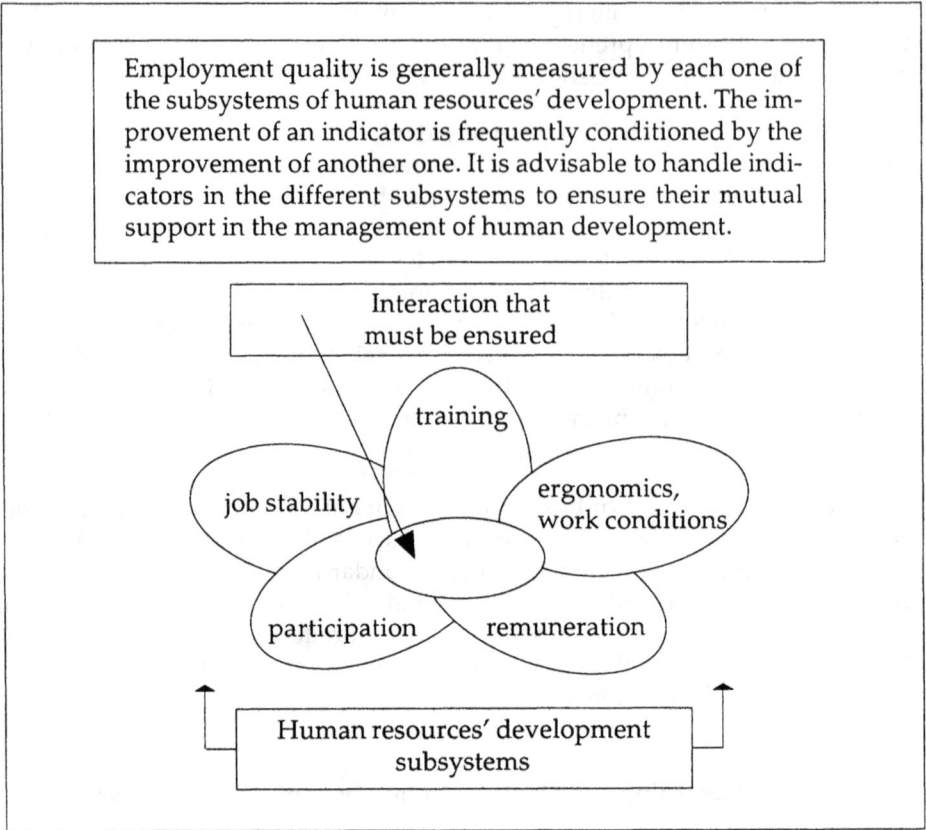

Another principle is the necessary connection that learning must keep with practice. This has the advantage that efforts are always justified by the fulfilment of an objective or need. The difficulty for organisations is that the trajectory of learning results is less clear-cut when learning is defined as a process wherein knowledge is created through the transformation of experience (Kolb, 2000). In this case, the ultimate experience is the competitiveness position of the organisation.

Having an experimental connotation, in this definition knowledge and occupational competency are envisaged as transformation processes, constantly created and recreated, instead of independent entities to be acquired and transmitted. This process of creating and recreating knowledge and competencies through learning refers to the two dimensions of knowledge and competencies: their objective and subjective aspects, what is tacit and what is explicit.

A third element conditioning the learning capacity of organisations is as-sessment of the improvement of decent work in them (employment quality). En-quiries among personnel members, effective communication, shared informa-tion and involvement help to create the mutual trust and understanding, shared values and goals that are required for concerted organisational learning actions (Tolentino, 2000).

This is yet another example that decent work is a concept whose compo-nents are mutually reinforcing. Social dialogue, one of the four dimensions of decent work and *sine qua non* condition for a job to merit the qualification of "decent", makes it possible for enterprises to attain maximum relevance between their training actions and the specific needs of an organisation which -as seen earlier- is a powerful factor for promoting work productivity.

A fourth element is the support and resources necessary for learning to oc-cur. An entity defining itself as a learning organisation will have to bring about a social, organisational and technical environment conducive to learning, based on facilities and structures supporting personal development (Warner, 2001). After all, knowledge is generated by and through persons.

2
TRAINING AND ORGANISATIONAL LEARNING

The model described in the preceding section is a simplified picture placing concepts in a strategic outline, which enables us to justify training policies and programmes. We still need to develop the tools to shape a training strategy. In order to bridge the gap between the conceptual framework and the concrete training tools, we have resorted to the identification of the critical variables affecting the relationship between training and productivity. Those critical values are derived from an analysis of concrete contents, within the terms of reference of the conceptual frame.

One first important aspect of contexts is the greater interconnection of markets, and consequently the greater number of competitors enterprises have to face. The results are higher and more constant pressures to adapt to manifold market behaviours. Another consequence is the need for differentiation based on the organisations' intangible capacities, eg. those that are intrinsic in them and difficult to copy.

Another important aspect of contexts is the nature of new technologies, especially information, communication and organisational management technologies. The architecture of these technologies is open-ended and they contribute to the improvement of productivity and competitive advantage insofar as they are adapted to the specific needs of organisations.

A third important element is the declining price of one of the key inputs for productivity: information, mainly through electronic communications media. It is the main source in the generation of new knowledge, although not a sufficient factor, for information requires an intellectual (cognitive) process of understanding to turn into knowledge. "Information has value because someone has given it context, sense and a particular interpretation. It is a unique contribution in knowledge, ability and perspective, a highly subjective process that in the best of cases only can be facilitated by technology" (Cross; Israelit, 2000).

Organisational learning in the current context

"It is the effort to increase the fundamental intellect of the organisation day by day. To encourage personnel to learn because the excitement and energy they get from learning is enormous and it gives energy to the organisation (...) A learning environment must be promoted in work teams, where the sky is the limit (...) a struggle has to be fought every day against the bureaucracy that restricts learning (...) personal attitudes have to be banished such as "I know nine things and will teach you eight" and replaced by "I will teach you nine things today, and a tenth one tomorrow morning."

J. Welch, former General Electric CEO, quoted in TechLearn TRENDS, N° 223, 28 November 2001, and in Latham, 2001.

A fourth relevant aspect is the growing concern and pressure of civil society about effects on the natural environment and working conditions, resulting from market deregulation and increasing competition. With the support of the mass media and a message of significance for the expectations of civil society, fundamental human rights have become a parameter to judge the behaviour of organisations in the context of globalisation. Both through State taxing mechanisms and forms of market self-regulation that have emerged -(like the codes of conduct for socially responsible companies, supervised by civil society organisations)- many aspects of decent work are now being included in the agenda of organisational learning.[9] This kind of liability is also connected with the capacity for generating decent work.

Faced with a threat of loss of image with consumers, that in the last resort are the end users of the goods and services offered, companies operating in the consumer market of clients with high purchasing power have had to accept a commitment with decent work and other fundamental rights.

In the sphere of decent work, what generally gets priority attention are labour rights. Although there is still a conceptual discussion going on as to which labour rights must necessarily be present in a definition of decent work, a consensus already exists (and socially responsible enterprises are very careful about it) that at least the principles embodied in the fundamental ILO conventions must be

---

9 The garment industry in export processing zones of developing countries, like the Dominican Republic, Mexico and Central America, has been increasingly made to comply with social codes of conduct issued by their wholesale traders, holders of leading brands. Compliance is ensured through labour audits carried out by independent certifying agencies recognised by civil society.

respected, referring to: a) freedom of association, trade union freedom and effective recognition of the right of collective bargaining; b) banishment of all forms of forced or compulsive labour; c) effective eradication of child labour, and c) elimination of discrimination in employment and work.

These aspects have altered the traditional relation between training and productivity. In this new context productivity is seen as the result not only of the learning efforts of the group of "knowledge employees" in an organisation, but as the outcome of a collective learning endeavour by the organisational community. In this scheme, constantly learning and helping others to learn is a task shared by all personnel, including operatives. The aim is not only to share knowledge, but above all to create it.

Training of the working personnel is no longer seen as a closed cycle, whose main objective is incorporating individuals into the technological and organisational parameters of productive processes. The involvement of all employees as actors and not mere objects of change and organisational learning, makes the difference with the traditional approach to innovation and learning.

The novel aspect of this approach is the importance awarded to the tacit knowledge of employees, the uncoded know-how for carrying out functions and fulfilling objectives. Tacit knowledge is nowadays considered to be the main source of knowledge in organisations. The challenge is to tap this source by means of a collective goal, motivating personnel members to share, explain and try out their implicit knowledge consisting of experiences, feelings, associations, intuitions and assumptions (Weggeman, 1997). The wider this knowledge activation mechanism spreads, the greater its benefits will be for organisational learning and development.

In this perspective, employees will have to be constantly motivated to look for information and keep updated through other persons or computerised systems. The process encompasses all personnel, it is not sufficient to send down memos or explanatory notes from the management level. Employees have to assimilate the information and need time to understand it in relation to their own reality. It is only when they have had the opportunity to conclude that the changes in work systems are important, that knowledge will have been transferred and learning will occur about such changes.

Learning organisations are those where a collective learning process takes place. This is a situation in which several persons belonging to the same group employ themselves in individually or interactively enriching their knowledge in the same subject area or domain (Weggeman, 1997). This does not mean that they all learn the same things, or that the results of their learning are the same. Differences in information, experiences, abilities and attitudes will lead to a differentiation in ways of observing and interpreting.

From the organisations' point of view, their interest is to induce behaviour patterns consistent with objectives laid down, producing a shared mental attitude that may improve and stimulate synergy among group members (ibidem). The important thing is that the learning process should point in the direction of what the organisation needs in a broad sense, including the employees' needs. To reconcile both needs, the self- awareness of personnel members should be focalised, clarifying the role and responsibilities that each one of them has in the organisation (Latham, 2001).

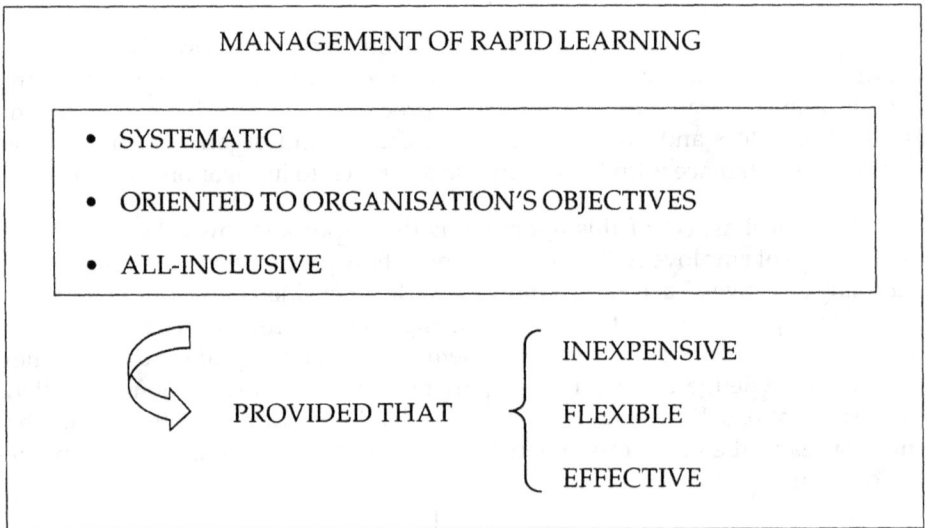

MANAGEMENT OF RAPID LEARNING

- SYSTEMATIC

- ORIENTED TO ORGANISATION'S OBJECTIVES

- ALL-INCLUSIVE

PROVIDED THAT
{ INEXPENSIVE
FLEXIBLE
EFFECTIVE

Long route strategy: Inclusive organisational learning

Present-day circumstances pressure organisations to adopt a learning strategy that in this paper we have called the long route, which channels personnel training towards the enhancement of productivity and competitiveness. Owing to the many points of screening and contingency prevention that exist along the road from the design of learning processes to their impact on productivity and competitiveness, a strategy will have to be defined for negotiating it.

The main objective is the accelerated learning of new knowledge in organisations, aiming at the sustained enhancement of productivity and competitiveness, based on the interaction between individual and collective learning, encouraged by a constant improvement of the quality of employment.

The learning strategy involves systematic efforts aiming at the general objectives of the organisation and including all its personnel. For the strategy to be viable in current contexts it must at least fulfil the requirements of low costs, flexible application and high impact.

Learning and knowledge generation efforts have to be strategically oriented. Unless they are focalised, organisations learn according to *mainstream* trends, evolving towards markets and capacities below optimal level. Tracking the surrounding environment and formulating active policies that acknowledge the importance of learning and knowledge, help to offset such trends.

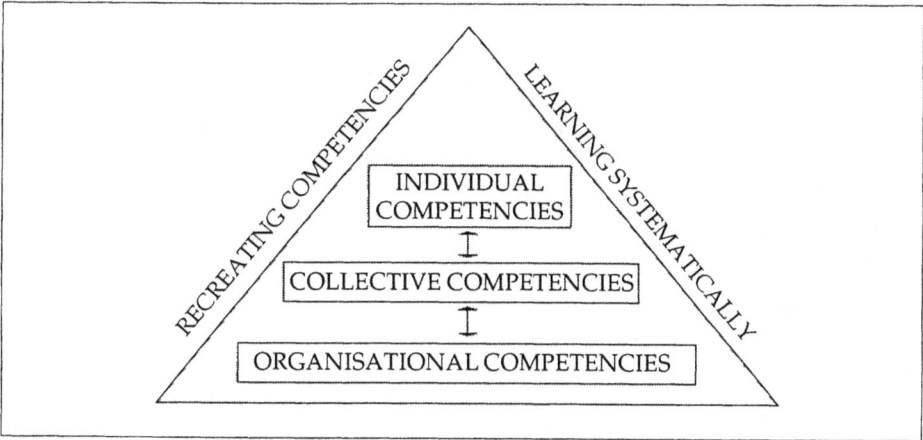

The key word is flexibility. "Organisations that learn quickly, at low cost and accurately are characterised by a high degree of flexibility in their operation, which distinguishes them form those that learn slowly, laboriously and expensively or are just destined not to learn at all. While inner momentum is a very functional characteristic for organisations in stable and foreseeable contexts, it can be extremely destructive when it prevents learning in moments of significant changes (Langlois; Robertson, 1996).

Flexibility is a prerequisite for training strategies to have an impact. Individual learning needs to migrate to collective, group level, and to organisational level through some type of social interaction. The important thing is to achieve learning that entails action, which means modifying and/or transforming existing processes through generated competencies. This calls for flexibility in learning processes and instruments.

Inversely, an organisation's context is subject to constant changes, which necessitates changes in the collective processes and competencies required, that in turn extend to individual competencies and learning. They are tides flowing in opposite directions, whose coordination requires organisational flexibility.

EFFECTIVENESS OF FORMAL AND INFORMAL LEARNING

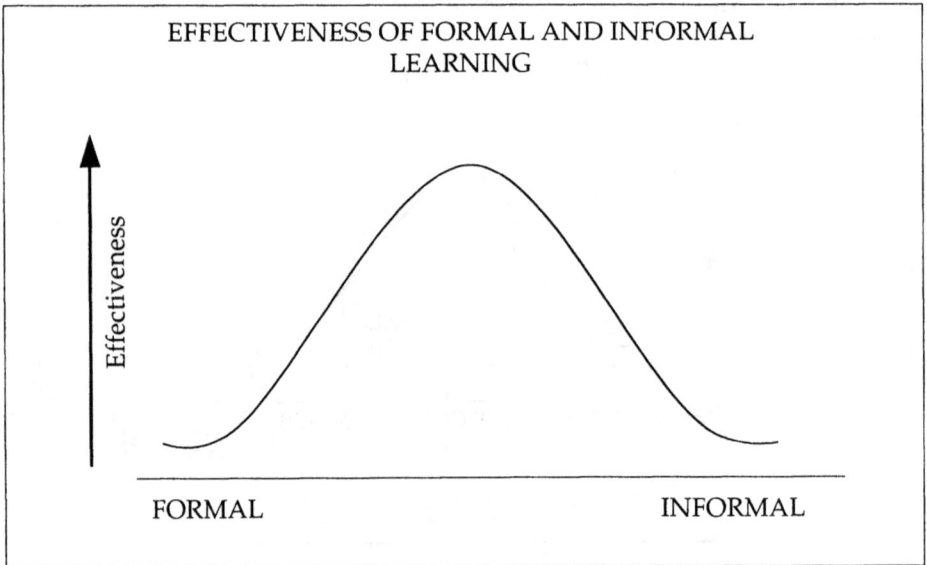

FORMAL INFORMAL

Informal learning manifests itself in many different ways in organisations. There are several challenges for influencing it effectively, that can be summarised as follows: informal training is complex, its results depend on its context and its management is difficult. In some cases workers have expectations of access to learning and occupational development through their job. In other cases they have few opportunities for learning and career development. The scenario becomes more depressing when they have few possibilities of occupational progress, and the feeling is reinforced by the low aspirations of their bosses (Rainbird, 2000).

The answer to the above is a flexible learning proposal responding from the training area to the requirements of a rapid, all-inclusive and effective learning strategy. To prevent that flexibility from weakening learning efforts, it is essential to anchor them in competencies aiming at productivity and competitiveness objectives. "An approach based on competencies helps organisations to identify and turn into goals important forms of knowledge, that are necessary for their future success. This is an important planning process, as critical knowledge is not developed in the course of everyday activities" (Cross; Israelit, 2000).

Flexible learning strategy

Flexible learning is closely connected to the way in which contemporary enterprises operate. It includes new approaches to the planning of training, its structure and contents, the methods it utilises and access to it. Training needs to centre on well defined applicable targets, and to go further in the development of legitimate and valid knowledge (Jakupec; Garrick, 2000).

Flexible learning is based on two parallel concepts: informal and formal learning. Flexible learning is the capacity of organisations for steering a course between formal and informal realms according to their own needs and convenience. The premise being that the effectiveness of an organisation's learning efforts increases insofar as it can manage to combine formal and informal procedures.

Organisations are beginning to recognise informal learning as a source of new knowledge and personnel development, and a strategic field for their training policies. In part because it allows them to cut down on training costs. But the most powerful reason is that it enables them to act upon intangible knowledge areas, that formal training cannot reach or can only cover in a limited way. This is a two-way channel between individuals and organisations. On the one hand, employees learn in their concrete work context, and on the other hand organisations gather together their individual potential and profit by it.

Formal training based on coded knowledge is too limited in scope and objectives in an economic context requiring dynamic organisations with distinctive market identities. This in no way means the disappearance of formal learning, but a limitation of its fields of action. It signifies that organisations will have to develop appropriate mechanisms and instruments for effectively influencing informal learning.

DEVELOPMENT OF KNOWLEDGE

Coded

Formal learning

Structured

Programmed
(place, time)

Non programmed
(place, time)

Unstructured

Uncoded

Informal learning

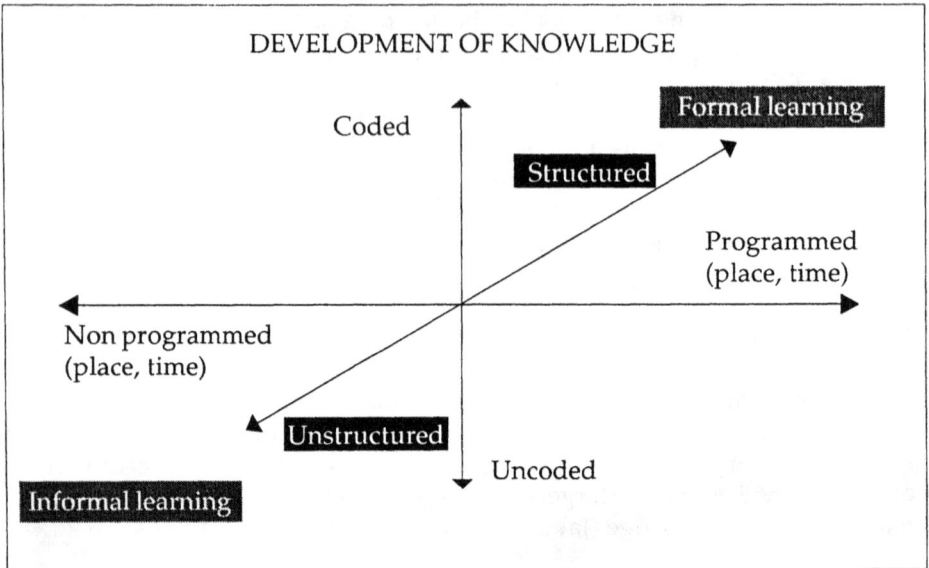

"As society becomes more complex, so do personnel training requirements, and there is growing demand for flexible learning. There is therefore an inverse relationship between the complexity of selection and the flexibility of learning. This is particularly so as on the one hand work becomes fragmented, and on the other there are unforeseeable changes.

Traditional divisions of labour vanish, differences become blurred between everyday life and work, between learning and working, the community and the enterprise.

Abilities are required for applying knowledge and experience in unfamiliar circumstances, and flexible learning offers fruitful and varied possibilities in that field".
(Jakupec; Garrick, 2000)

Informality denotes that neither the contents, place, form or persons involved in the learning process are predetermined. The management of informal learning emphasises self-organisation and self-determination.

As frequently stated, the idea is not to replace formal by informal learning but to give the latter a much more explicit place than it has been assigned traditionally. Both formal and informal learning modes are often not very effective in their ultimate expression (totally formal or totally informal). It is preferable to combine the two, perhaps leaning slightly towards the informal side. In some occasions the contents of the learning process are not predetermined, in others its place or the personnel taking part in it. Going to extremes – a complete absence of predetermination, or predetermination of the whole learning process – is not considered an effective strategy.

From the viewpoint of managing rapid and effective learning, informality ensures success, for it guarantees the flexibility, low cost and impact of the learning efforts. The other aspects of speedy learning are covered by its formal component: the systematic part of the process, orienting it towards the organisation's objectives, specially client satisfaction, and coverage of all the personnel.

Informal learning has *flexibility* because the purpose, place and participants in the process are not predetermined in a rigid manner. Flexibility in the management of learning is required to be consistent with the progression of change in the organisation of processes and work. Nevertheless, there are also structural aspects of substance that do not necessarily change rapidly, like basic procedures, for example. Learning such aspects acquires more formal dimensions, especially for those who come to an organisation or job for the first time.

The balance between formality and informality refers not only to the contents but to the place and space where learning takes place. It is a topic that has given rise to polemics in connection with new learning techniques, like multimedia and the Internet.

For example, learning via *internet or intranet* is characterised by its capacity to offer contents exactly at the moment when they are required, which the traditional planning of classroom courses does not have. It is also flexible in the adaptation of contents, rapid and of low cost considering the number of persons it can reach, and allows for learning at a personalised tempo (Festa, 2000).

However, these advantages do not make this training technique displace the traditional ones. To determine which training technique is most effective we must first understand how persons and organisations learn. It is essential for the success of a training programme to ensure that the training media or techniques are in consonance with the abilities to be developed (ibidem).

> *"Training by means of the Internet or Intranet works better when it is used as a complement to traditional techniques. For instance, it is ideal for getting students acquainted with the theory before practising it in a group or class environment. When all participants have devoted some time to reviewing the relevant information on the internet or intranet before the lesson, they will start the practical session with some notion of basic principles, and will all have a similar level of knowledge. This will enable facilitators to develop the trainees' knowledge, as they already have a grounding of basic principles".* (Festa, 2000).

There are situations in which training techniques can only be applied in a group or schoolroom environment. For example, interaction with other persons is a significant technique for understanding and appropriating the required abilities and knowledge. It enables several persons with similar experiences to agree about how to relate coded knowledge to real work situations, and even to extrapolate conclusions to other situations that had initially not been contemplated in the coding. This offers transcendental learning opportunities for organisations.

Consequently, any training programme that omits direct contact among students runs the risk that they will spend their time and efforts relating to the machine instead of other persons. Group techniques, the possibility of collaborating with other learners and practising a technique are very valuable learning tools that cannot be replaced by the machine (ibidem).

To attain the objective of making learning more effective in the context of constant change that organisations have to live with, the proposal of replacing or recombining formal by informal training seems too simple. Between the formal and the informal there is a wide range of options and modes, blending aspects characterised as formal with other, informal ones. Optimal learning efficiency lies probably in one or another of these combinations.

The main thing about the proposal is that it breaks away from the idea that learning processes are necessarily conservative and tend to reinforce existing frames of reference, reinforcing only the knowledge already incorporated into the organisation. Much more difficult and less accepted is a strategy aimed at attaining a qualitatively higher level of knowledge, transcending and transforming what already exists. Part of this strategy is to motivate employees to move in the direction of such transcendental or transformation learning (Weggeman, 1997).

Transcendental learning consists of processes in which individuals and/or organisations are capable to reflect in action upon the practice undertaken. This is called "reflection in action". The knowledge thus generated goes beyond what already exists in the organisation, i.e. current explicit and tact knowledge. This self-transcendental knowledge reflects the energy driving new know-how in the organisation, and consequently, the strategic value it has. Regarding the other two areas of knowledge, explicit knowledge represents reflection without action, while tacit knowledge is reflection after action (Sharmer, 2001).

The consequences for training are significant. We may suggest that an initial step in the direction of transcendental knowledge is to set in motion the capabilities and know-how that are frozen inside he organisation. To that end, a great deal of attention has to be paid to the subjective nature of learning and the idiosyncrasy of all the personnel involved, to the social and individual processes of learning in the organisational context. "What we learn is closely connected with the conditions in which we learn" (Brown; Duguid, 2000).

It will be necessary to recognise and promote the subjectiveness of individuals in the workplace. To visualise employees as active learners but also as self-regulating subjects that wish, think, feel and act; that strive to reconcile their own objectives with those of the enterprise.

Learning to be flexible and self–regulated imply a number of values and attitudes leading to adaptability, constant modification and acceptance of the fluency between certainty and uncertainty as a permanent precondition for subjectivity. A contingent rather than monolithic subjectivity, in constant change, forever finding answers and obstacles. Autonomy, self-management and individual responsibility, so that persons can make their own project out of their workplace and furnish added value to the organisation (Usher, 2000).

Management of the learning process must help persons to learn in an effective way and concentrate on the social processes that turn knowledge into action. In other words, not to confine learning to individuals but make sure that it is applied at the level of the organisation.

What does this mean in terms of curricula, teaching material, teaching methods, participative practices, financial and administrative procedures? These questions do not yet have definitive answers. Collective, homogeneous conventional courses can hardly meet the needs of people with different life stories, at different stages in their career and in differing economic branches and sectors. The ensuing queries are: how to be flexible with learners? and how can trainees be made to learn flexibly? Trainees or learners are the customers; their needs and contexts must be understood. Nevertheless, learners have to be taught how to be flexible in their learning process, how to utilise teaching materials, how to plan and prepare themselves for study, to use computers, etc. (Evans, 2000).

Two points seem to be fundamental in the search for answers to these questions. The first one is that the curriculum of flexible learning derives from work and not disciplinary knowledge. Both capacity and knowledge are flexible in connection with contents. This leads to a shift from theoretical and disciplinary knowledge towards knowledge related to problem solving. Training by competencies, that we will describe further on, stems from the concept of curricula based on practice.

The second point is that the subjectivity of learners is more forceful in the transforming learning model. It would be over-simplistic to think that all the personnel in an organisation is likely to be equally motivated, inspired and prepared to play the role of learners, ready to take active part in the process of generation and application of transcendental knowledge. And this, for a number of reasons, some of them internal policy motives, others caused by adverse intuitions and/or feelings, others through the insecurity of feeling ridiculous or the fear of losing a safe or privileged position, and others yet by the sheer fatigue and exhaustion of learning.

According to Edgar H. Schein, the well known researcher in organisational learning, it is not infrequent to see that 80% of the personnel in an organisation behave passively and only react to the coercion of management or a critical market situation. They rationalise the effort and weariness of learning and learn just what they are supposed to know. The remaining 20% are persons who always feel the need to take action: about half of them will actively support the suggestions made by the management or by the group that has taken the lead in transforming the learning model; the other half will take any kind of action to oppose the proposals (Coutu, 2002).

Therein lies the challenge for managing the sort of training intended to have an effect on productivity. "We know how to improve the learning of an individual or a work team, but we do not know how to intervene systematically in the collective culture to prompt a transforming learning process throughout an organisation" (ibidem).

Paradoxically, according to Schein, effort, exhaustion and coercion seem to be at the root of the learning progression, both for individuals and organisations. The process of unlearning habits, customs and practices that have ceased to be valid can be very painful. Learners will accept that effort and "pain" provided that the fear of apprehending something new is less than the fear or concern of "surviving" economically and socially in the organisation (ibidem).

Insofar as training management may succeed in dispelling fears by creating a safe and reliable environment for unlearning some things and relearning others, it will stimulate the process. Many organisations will try to encourage learning by increasing the fear of "survival" in their personnel, because it is the easiest way. According to Schein, this is completely wrong because it often awakens resistance, an attitude of "wait and see" in the personnel, faced with the many reorganisation plans presented by management to keep up the "pressure" on them (ibidem).

The opposite also applies: management has to gain credibility by fostering a healthy and positive desire to learn in a psychologically safe learning environment. There will always be resistance to learning, but once employees have accepted the need to learn, the process can be facilitated by means of good teaching materials, group support, feedback, surveys, etc. Stress must be laid on the validity of what is being taught. Insofar as validity is justified and workers feel at ease with the learning process, coercive persuasion will appear to be not only effective but also legitimate (ibidem).

This support/resistance dynamics among personnel regarding application of the transforming learning instruments that we describe below is partly due, on the one hand to the combination of effort and pain that learning implies, and on the other to the concern for survival within the organisation. However, over and above this is the psychological safety that individuals should feel in applying such instruments. When workers with minimal schooling levels feel safe to give opinions, ask questions and raise objections in the presence of engineers/middle managers, the latter have to make an effort to unlearn and leave aside prejudices that workers are ignorant. At this point, pressure on middle managers is necessary by facilitators and high management, as otherwise a psychologically safe atmosphere could not be created for workers.[10]

---

10 The socio-psychological mechanism is much more complex. Workers can suffer reprisals from middle managers for their participation in transforming learning initiatives, in which case pressures from high management or project leaders have no effect. In the cases analysed in this paper it also happens that one or several workers may take advantage of a lack of leadership of middle managers to question their decisions and cause splits among them. Another situation is that the interests of some workers coincide with those of some middle managers to keep certain problems or dysfunctions in the dark (for example privileges or overtime).

3

METHODOLOGICAL PRINCIPLES: PRODUCTIVITY MEASUREMENT AND ENHANCEMENT SYSTEM (ProMES) AND SELF-TRAINING AND ASSESSMENT GUIDES BY COMPETENCIES (STAG)

These two methodologies are centred on learning processes that directly involve working personnel. The stress laid on workers does not mean that the rest of the organisation is left aside. Middle managers are essential in operating the model. They have to learn how to train workers and follow up the improvement proposals that may be made. Some studies have shown that learning on the job may be facilitated or hampered by: a) the organisation of work and the assignment of enriched tasks; b) the social climate of the work environment (Eraut *et.al.* 1997).

Application of the proposed model implies a cognitive, attitudinal and emotional learning process for middle and upper managers.

Cognitive learning refers to the technical aspects of managing the model, application of its analytical capabilities for studying problems, preparation of training materials and sessions and the adoption of commitments.

The attitudinal learning process of middle managers begins by recognising the importance of contributions by workers and accepting, if justified, their criticism of middle management. They must be able to strike a balance between the objectives of the organisation and those of the workers. They have to handle and channel the requests of workers.

They have to accept the fact that workers can take over some of the tasks so far performed by middle managers. All this demands of them an inclination to

45

devote energy and time to the job, and accepting that their role has to change from supervising and implementing to facilitating and training. Socially, it requires an attitude of preaching with the example in everything concerning personal safety implements and respect for safety standards, as well as cleanliness and order in working areas.[11]

The emotional learning process of middle managers is their capacity for encouraging workers to learn, motivating them to take part in feedback board meetings and to study training guidelines. It is also their capacity to control their repressive and negative emotions towards workers in everyday activities, establishing an atmosphere of mutual trust and direct communication with them. Middle managers must be sensitive to the feelings of the workers in their charge, and react to them in a way that may reconcile their expectations to the values of the organisation.

These two methodologies coordinate training with the improvement of productivity in different manners. The **Productivity Measurement and Enhancement System (ProMES)** begins with participative group monitoring of productivity and employment quality indicators. From such reflections actions emerge that have direct bearing on group processes and performances. In periodic meetings of critical analysis of results, training processes emerge based on explicit and tacit knowledge. Informal learning occurs in non-predetermined training contents, and also in the fact that the critical issues at each board meeting are not always shared and analysed by the same personnel. The formal component is expressed through the programming of feedback board meetings, the periodical measurement and follow-up of the improvement commitments adopted.

The advantage of ProMES is that it starts almost immediately at the level of operational workers. Short term impacts are generally achieved through improvements in procedures and communication resulting from organisational learning. The disadvantage is that there is no follow-up of individual learning and performance. A personal commitment is not generated in each worker for the development of the competencies required in the necessary depth. In the case of sugar mills, ProMES does not guarantee that each worker will know how to interpret correctly critical process parameters (pressures, temperatures, speeds) or will be aware of the consequences of any parameter being outside the allowed range.

---

11 "The development of middle and upper managers usually emphasises motivation, productivity and evaluation but pays little attention to supporting the learning process of subordinates, the organisation of work, assignment of tasks and creating a work environment that may promote informal learning. This imbalance may derive from lack of knowledge about real and possible learning in the workplace" (Eraut *et.al*, 1997).

Self-training and Assessment Guides (STAG) are based on training in explicit knowledge, derived from productive practices, and aim at developing competencies individually. They are complemented by performance assessments. The sum of the two plus associated knowledge develop the required competencies in workers. In a second stage, STAGs are combined with indicators of organisational productivity improvements, and with proposals for upgrading processes, to consolidate the impact of training on the organisation and secure constant feedback into the learning process.

Informal assessment is involved because the way in which guidelines are handled and the date and manner of the assessments are not predetermined. The formal part are the coded contents of the guidelines and previously devised checklists.

The advantage of guides is that they allow for individual follow-up of the workers' learning process and in consequence the commitment of each worker to the learning effort. The disadvantage is that start-up is slow, because the design of instruments takes a long time. Several months usually elapse, sometimes one year, before getting through to workers. Another disadvantage is that organisational learning is not always ensured. It is relatively easy to concentrate on the learning of each individual, overlooking the solution of common problems. For example in sugar mills the care and handling of tools is first of all an organisational problem requiring new rules of collective behaviour (placing tools in visible and accessible places, not removing them from the plant, not keeping them in personal boxes). It cannot be resolved individually or by means of study guides or performance checklists.

The two methodologies are proposed for an effective training that may affect and modify the work culture in the direction of a learning organisation. Effective training is based as much on the needs of the organisation as on those of its personnel. "Understanding the results expected by the personnel is understanding why they do what they do. When we have managed to change their expectations, we will have changed their behaviour. Training must be explicit as to what employees must *stop doing, begin to do or continue doing* to contribute to the organisation's strategy" (Latham, 2001). Undertaking a process of that kind is not a theoretical problem, but above all a cultural one.

The culture of work is the way in which employees act out and understand the everyday reality of work and their role in it, on the basis of common aspects that generate similar behaviour patterns *vis-à-vis* specific situations. It is also the way in which enterprises visualise personnel within their strategy. This view is conditioned by the existing work culture, eg. by the values, beliefs, tacit conventions, cognitive structures and explicit strategies that involve a number of shared meanings among personnel, which allows for the "building of a social reality" within the enterprise embodying a system of "mental habits" in its personnel (Schoenberger, 1997). But it also depends on the strategy that enterprises pursue. Corporate strategy and work culture are interrelated dimensions.

Work culture and communication cannot be conceived as separate phenomena within an organisation but as indissolubly intertwined. Which means that attempting to change the work culture implies changing the forms and contents of communication in the organisation. Communication oriented towards knowing how to listen and to mutual commitment. This proposal is the axis round which the ProMES proposal and application of the self-training and evaluation guidelines revolve.

Changing the work culture aims at meeting new market needs, technological and organisational innovations. It means attempting to change the values embedded in a solid and consistent network of beliefs and notions that tend to maintain the *status quo* (Schoenberger, 1997). Consequently, it is not a rapid or straightforward process, as it meets various levels and types of resistance.

Management of change in the work culture breaking up with accepted trends implies knowing how to identify and counteract areas of resistance.[12] This is an important task in managing the all-inclusive learning model. The important thing here is to achieve a lasting change of attitudes, where persuasion by knowledge is not enough (or direct action by punishment or sanction). "If there is no conviction or true change of attitudes and values, long-term lasting behaviour can hardly be achieved. (…) ways of influencing attitudes and values are connected with participation schemes. The problem is that such schemes are slower to implant although they ensure better long-term results, as they are the foundation for personal improvement and development in the organisation" (Ronco, Lladé, 2000).

The two methodologies are distinguished by having their moment of truth, the point at which they strike a chord that operates coactively but at the same time wears down resistance to the effort and fear of learning. ProMES, systematic measurement and follow-up, build up collective pressure in the direction of compliance and improvement, relying on *esprit de corps* or competitions between groups or shifts of workers. For example, in sugar mills, the groups themselves

---

12 Work culture is not static, nor is it always resistant to change. It is in a process of fluency and constant transformation as a result of new problems, contradictions and trends. It has a power and conflict dimension, and the type of change selected depends on how conflicts are solved in practice. Processes of change in the work culture always have a component that derives from the path that was being followed, and another one that breaks away from that path (Schoenberger, 1997).

pressure members to use personal protection equipment (helmet, gloves) because omission to do so is directly reflected in the scores they are awarded.

In the case of guides and performance assessment instruments, self assessment helps to allay fears and resistance and is also an initial moment of truth in developing a commitment with learning. Subsequent assessments and follow-up encourage learners to persist in their efforts, as they clearly perceive that they are necessary. At the same time, the procedure is coercive as it immediately detects attitudes of personal resistance and brings negative consequences in the organisation for the individuals concerned.

There is still an important question pending, that relates to the whys and wherefores of these methodologies. How is the culture of work.before and after the changes? To answer this question we must clarify that the culture of work is not static, it is constantly undergoing a process of change along a certain path (Schoenberger, 1997). The change that we mean here is a change of path.

The answer to this question depends on the view we have of the characteristics of learning in a competitive enterprise in the present-day context. The broad view of "before and after" stems from the dysfunctionality and lack of effectiveness of rigid and unilateral hierarchical structures, direct supervision and repetitive tasks requiring routine skills, where knowledge is created in a disciplined and coded manner, and validated by a disciplined community. The nature and progress of information and computer sciences, and of biotechnology in the case of agribusiness and pharmaceutical industries, the increasing occurrence of unforeseen situations and the demands of markets for meeting customer needs more explicitly, have eroded the effectiveness of this model of organisational learning.

The "after" is the picture that should provide an answer to these new requirements. It is self-governed teamwork, with personnel equipped with generic competencies or qualifications of a higher level, capable of working in an environment of learning and generation of contextual knowledge. That is to say, an environment in which knowledge is produced because it is useful for a concurrent work situation. The sources of specialised knowledge are various and manifold, but significant contexts for their application are defined by market processes. This calls for an "educated" labour force, having learned not only skills but "right" attitudes, dispositions and inclinations – and in this context the term "right" refers above all to flexibility (Usher, 2000).

a. ProMES Model

The Productivity Measurement and Enhancement System (ProMES) was originally developed by Pritchard and co-workers of the Psychology Department of Texas University (Pritchard, 1990).

The ProMES model is based on the assumption that if the personnel in an organisation adequately modify their attitudes, productivity increases. This assertion is based on another more general assumption, eg. that the behaviour of personnel in an organisation has an important impact on productivity. In the last resort, it is the personnel that puts technological and administrative systems to productive use.

How can behaviour be modified? And, in what direction does it have to be modified? Changes in motivation, information and knowledge modify behaviour. The direction of that change embodies the objectives to be pursued by the organisation and its different departments, channelling individual efforts towards a collective result.

A sustained improvement of productivity based on changes in personnel behaviour is not the result of a single action but of a process of interlocked actions. Behaviour is not changed in one fell swoop. It is rooted in mental representations and their respective meanings, in customs and routines, beliefs and power relationships. A change of behaviour is a process that follows a course with rate and direction, which does not necessarily mean linear progress: there are reversals, detours and hitches along the way.

Regarding the *rate* of changes in behaviour, the challenge for organisations is to find anchors preventing the process to go back, and propelling it forward. Changes have to be institutionalised as organisational policy and culture, and also go deeper in the modification of behaviour. This can only be attained through the assimilation of new knowledge. To begin with, this is done by sharing good practices and know-how with co-workers, middle and upper managers. At a subsequent stage it will be necessary to analyse problems at their very origin, using a methodology that taps knowledge beyond what exists in the organisation. The methodology implies that the proposal resulting from an analysis has to be corroborated in practice, with the consequent readjustments that will in turn have to be evaluated, until a point is reached when the process can be closed, or when it remains in the same position, with the support of constant monitoring.[13]

---

13 The Toyota Company developed a scientific method that is applied at workers' level to analyse and solve problems and take advantage of opportunities. Its cornerstone is experimentation, that is in turn the basis for organising learning (Spear; Bowen, 1999).

Regarding the *direction* of behavioural change, the challenge for organisations is getting all their collaborators to work and learn in line with their manifest strategic and social objectives. For objectives to become an instrument of motivation, it is necessary but not sufficient that collaborators know about them and are kept informed about their progress and problems. All aspects of the objectives that collaborators may influence and control will have to be singled out and focalised. All important aspects of each area or function will also have to be underscored, for human attention tends to concentrate on what is measured. For example, when quantity, quality and accidents at work are important, all three aspects will have to be measured and results integrated into a single total or general indicator, denoting whether progress is being made. In this manner it becomes an instrument that motivates without deflecting the path of the process (Ibidem).

In its most elementary expression, productivity is the relation between input and output. In the case of personnel, the input is human energy. Productivity is higher in proportion to the intelligence, knowledge, ability and attitude with which that energy is applied, which results in performance. It is important to point out that producing more by consuming more human energy does not result in higher productivity, but in higher labour intensiveness. What ProMES seeks is to direct and process human energy so as to improve the outcome of labour, in terms of objectives achieved.

The generation of human energy applied to the work process is not unwavering. Mental and cognitive processes intervene that enhance it differently in people, both qualitatively and quantitatively. Such processes are directly related with learning and motivation. For that reason, success in managing the ProMES model depends on the capacity for exerting positive influence on workers, and promoting their willingness to make a constant learning effort.

DEFINITION OF INDICATORS

Name of indicator

Effectiveness

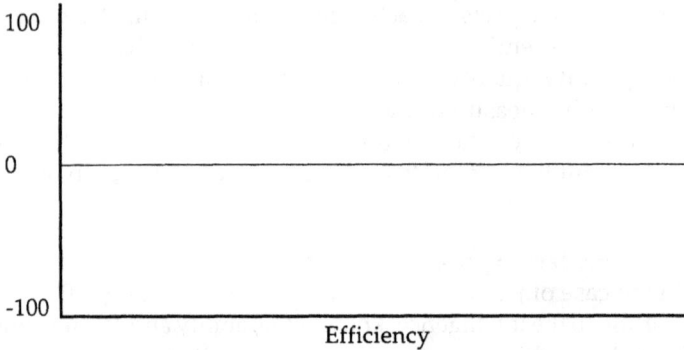

100

0

-100

Efficiency

Indicator		Max.	Neither good nor bad	Min.
	Effectiveness points	100	0	-100
	Value of indicator			

Methodological aspects of ProMES

For the model to have a sustained impact on personnel motivation and learning, several methodological aspects have to be complied with. The first one is that it must be circumscribed to aspects of organisational productivity that workers can control. This is a fundamental point, because it enables the feedback of measurement results to induce commitments to change in personnel behaviour.

EVALUATION OF MEASUREMENTS

> How do we reach
> intermediate points?

Once the extremes and point "0" have been set,
members of the group are asked how they
would assess an improvement from 160 tons/ an hour
to 167 tons/ an hour. The group will answer
according to the degree of difficulty and on
the basis of their experience. In this case,
they awarded it 60 points. This means that the
relationship between effectiveness and the
indicator need not be linear.

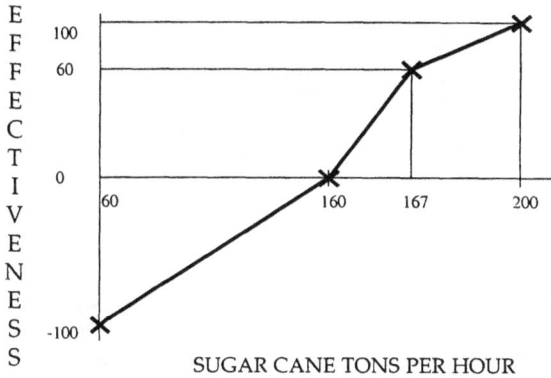

E
F
F
E
C
T
I
V
E
N
E
S
S

100
60
0
-100

60   160   167   200

SUGAR CANE TONS PER HOUR

The second methodological aspect is that the different objectives of the function to be performed by workers have to be measured. There is a tendency for workers to focus on what they are measuring, and pay less attention to tasks they are not measuring but that are nonetheless important. For that reason, measurement indicators must cover main personnel functions, that in the case of sugar refineries include not only qualitative and quantitative operational parameters, but issues of cleanliness, order and safety.

The third methodological aspect is that there should exist the possibility of assessing the measurement of indicators in some non-linear fashion. In other words, the relationship between efficiency and effectiveness is not necessarily linear; there may be different gradations according to the degree of difficulty for focusing energy on a given objective. For example, instead of concentrating all their energy on achieving the maximum possible reduction of fuel consumption in boiler areas, workers also strive for the conservation of steam power generation, as well as maintaining cleanliness, order and safety.

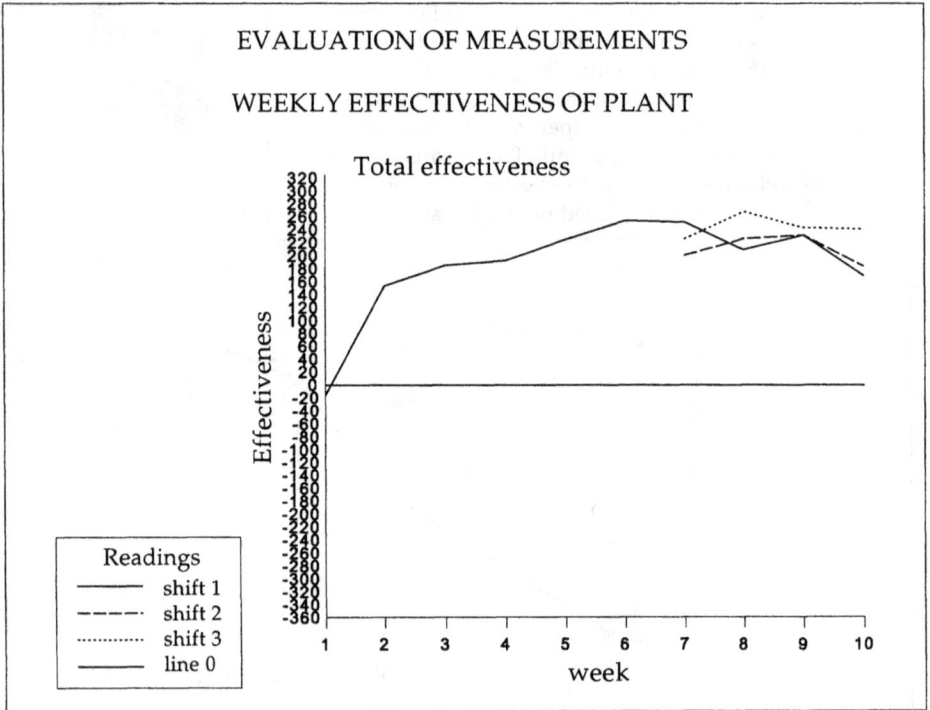

EVALUATION OF MEASUREMENTS

WEEKLY EFFECTIVENESS OF PLANT

The fourth methodological aspect regarding motivation is that there should exist the possibility of building a principal or aggregate indicator summarising progress in personnel performance, considering different and sometimes contradictory objectives. For example, maximising quantity and quality simultaneously is not a linear equilibrium; there will be a point where quality is jeopardised by producing more. In the case of ProMES this summarising indicator is constructed by standardising measurements on the basis of a single reference: effectiveness. It provides a standard showing how far the different objectives of the organisation are being met.

FOLLOW-UP OF IMPROVEMENT PROPOSALS				
ZUCARMEX CIA AZUCARERA LA FE, S A de CV	FIRST FEEDBACK MEETING	DATE CROP	01 AND 02 MARCH 2001-2002	
Nº	PROBLEM	SOLUTION	RESPONSIBLE	DEADLINE	Implemen-tation
1	VARIATION IN CANE FEEDING RATE	STANDARDISE CRITERIA EXPLAINING INSTRUCTIONS MORE CLEARLY	FOREMAN-WORKMAN TEAM	01-Mar.-02	
2	TIME LOST DUE TO DAMAGES IN Nº4 CANE LEVELLER	PROPOSAL: REMOVE LEVEL-LER & PUT IN STAND IN Nº 3 CONVEYOR TO PUSH CANE	Mr .JORGE	13 Feb.-02	
3	BLADES DAMAGED BY STONES & TRUNKS	INSTAL FOG LIGHTS TO IMPROVE VISIBILITY	Eng. BERNARDO	08 Mar.-02	
4	DIRTY AREA: SCRAP IRON & MAGNET PIECES	PLACE CONTAINER FOR SCRAP IRON etc.	Eng. IGNACIO & WORKTEAM	06 Mar.-02	
5	UNEVEN CANE FEEDING TO CONVEYORS	PLACE MARKING ON CONVEYORS	Eng. ADRIÁN	04 Mar.-02	
6	TRASH ON FLOORS	PLACE TRASH BINS IN MACHINES & MILLS AREA	Eng. IGNACIO & WORKTEAM	08 Mar.-02	
7	LACK OF CLEANING RAGS	SUPPLY CLEANING RAGS TO ALL AREAS	Eng. BERNARDO	03 Mar.-02	

The aggregate indicator shows synoptically the progress made in time and compares the performance of different groups of workers in the same or different departments. In sugar refineries comparisons are made between shifts in the same department, which induces "healthy" competition and is an extra motivation to those inherent in the model. However, this competition needs to be controlled to prevent "cannibalism" among workers of the same area or company.

The fifth methodological aspect is simple adaptation or change of indicators whenever necessary. This makes it possible to keep the system updated and to renew it without much difficulty, adapting it to changes of strategy. Readjustments of the model are also useful for sustaining the interest and motivation of workers.

In the sixth place, the model is straightforward and easily handled. This enables all workers to understand what is being measured and to take part in the daily collection of data. The model can be rapidly incorporated into the work culture and has immediate results. It can also be used in a variety of technological environments, from small workshops to large concerns.

ProMES AT BELLAVISTA REFINERY
1999-2000 CROP

AREA: MACHINERY & MILLS

WEEK	13

FROM: 22-MAR.00 TO: 28-MAR-00

Sac. IN BAGASSE

98-99 Crop Average 78.76

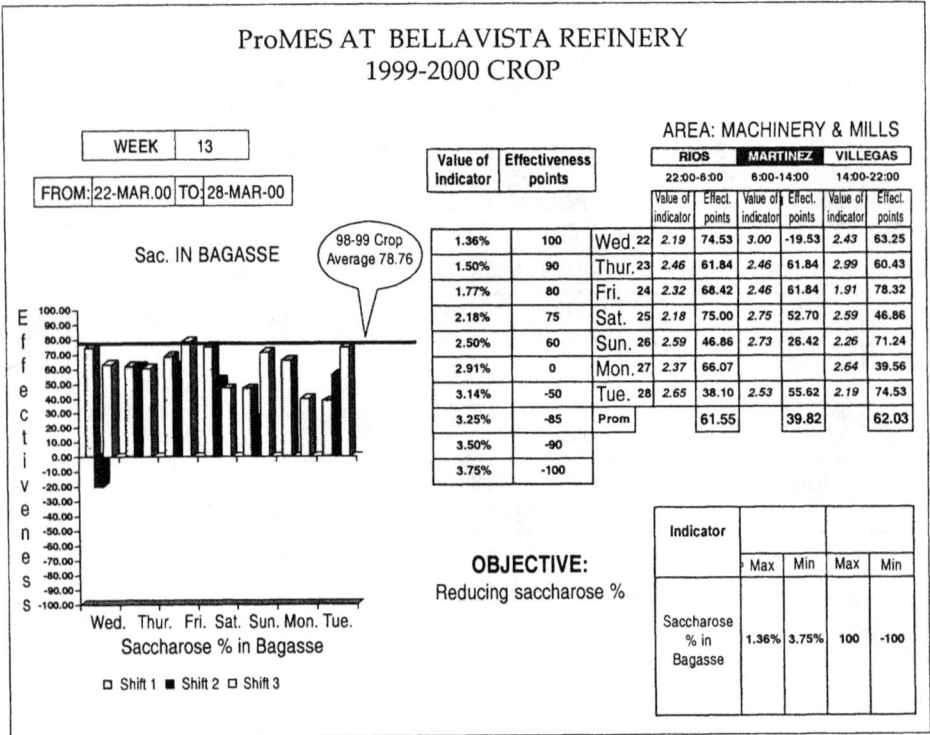

Wed. Thur. Fri. Sat. Sun. Mon. Tue.
Saccharose % in Bagasse

□ Shift 1 ■ Shift 2 □ Shift 3

Value of Indicator	Effectiveness points	Day	RIOS 22:00-6:00		MARTINEZ 6:00-14:00		VILLEGAS 14:00-22:00	
			Value of indicator	Effect. points	Value of indicator	Effect. points	Value of indicator	Effect. points
1.36%	100	Wed. 22	2.19	74.53	3.00	-19.53	2.43	63.25
1.50%	90	Thur. 23	2.46	61.84	2.46	61.84	2.99	60.43
1.77%	80	Fri. 24	2.32	68.42	2.46	61.84	1.91	78.32
2.18%	75	Sat. 25	2.18	75.00	2.75	52.70	2.59	46.86
2.50%	60	Sun. 26	2.59	46.86	2.73	26.42	2.26	71.24
2.91%	0	Mon. 27	2.37	66.07			2.64	39.56
3.14%	-50	Tue. 28	2.65	38.10	2.53	55.62	2.19	74.53
3.25%	-85	Prom		61.55		39.82		62.03
3.50%	-90							
3.75%	-100							

OBJECTIVE:
Reducing saccharose %

Indicator				
	Max	Min	Max	Min
Saccharose % in Bagasse	1.36%	3.75%	100	-100

The seventh aspect is the opening up of minds to critical reflection and systematisation through the feedback of measurements. A precondition for effective learning is a systematic effort of interaction, reflection and implementation of proposed improvements. Processing measurements with a standardised benchmark that permits comparisons in time, structures the learning process and lays the foundation for systematic efforts. Critical reflection through the cross-examination of operatives and middle managers is an important step in significant learning, that must be supplemented by other actions like the understanding of processes (concepts and generalisations), concrete experiences and evidence from the application of concepts to new situations. The follow-up of proposals for improvement and the commitment to adopt them is the anchoring mechanism through which learning materialises into action. This mechanism is an essential part of the model, for it documents and administers implementation of the proposals. It also helps to prioritise the activities to be undertaken.

Key sub-processes in the implementation of ProMES

Five key sub-processes have been identified.

The first one is to secure the support of high management, trade unions and middle managers for starting up the model. They have to be explained the principles of the model, the way in which they will take part, and the expected results.

The second process is to lay down a basis of personnel identification and confidence in the model, for example through the method of visualising the problem and its possible solutions. This methodology enables workers to voice their opinion and criticise working procedures, practices and conditions, especially communication mechanisms. This opening up of management to the workers gives legitimacy to the start-up of the model.

The third process consists of determining in which area application will begin. The objectives of this area or working group are identified, its respective indicators are established, and the scale of values for each indicator.

The fourth is systematic measuring, the processing and analysis of information and commitments by workers and management to achieve ongoing improvement.

The fifth step is adopting mechanisms for extending the model to other areas and ensuring its continuity.

These are the main stages for *expanding* the model. However, it must also be developed *in depth,* otherwise it runs the risk of stagnating and making no significant contribution to improved productivity.

The ProMES model aims at creating a shared mental representation of the objectives that the group of workers of the area in question must pursue. It includes all personnel in that area; it is not just a matter of sharing information and guidelines "from the top down" but precisely in the opposite direction, from the "bottom of the ladder upwards".

The methodological rationale of learning at ProMes feedback board meetings is similar to what is known as *Action Reflection Learning*, the principle of which is that group members are in a position to draw their own conclusions and get to conceptualisation and learning through reflection on action taken and problems to be solved. They share experiences and learning achievements. The implicit and explicit commitments stemming from that knowledge in turn lead them to a new cycle of activities, that constitute the object of further reflection. In this way the learning model is consolidated.

Individual and organisational learning alternate in ProMES in a "natural" manner, which has contributed to the acceptance and support of the system by all concerned (management, trade union, workers). It is worth noting that in individual learning the process of reflection has resulted in modifications of what some authors call the hidden curriculum (Usher, 2000). The environment and flexible dynamics of board meetings –where persons are taken into account as such, and workers are asked to give their opinions, critical comments and suggestions– promote in persons an attitude of collaboration, understanding, mutual respect and even adaptability to the changes that crop up.

However, after a while, the dynamics of ProMES at feedback boards may tend to decline through lack of blending of the knowledge derived from experience, socialisation and explanation, with that acquired rationally (from implicit to explicit knowledge). The proposal for counteracting this premature depletion of the model is going deeper at board meetings. This is similar to what is known in the literature as the *Research-Action* technique, complementary to *Action-Learning* and not unlike the problem-solving methods used at the Toyota Company (Solbek *et al*, 1998).

This proposal requires supervisors to play a qualitatively different role as coordinators or facilitators at board meetings. They are expected to prepare the meetings, which initially they were not supposed to do. They are also asked to focalise meetings on a single aspect or problem so as not to confuse or tire out workers. Instead of offering a technical explanation of a problem or process, the practice used at feedback boards is to ask questions centring on that problem or process, so that workers may voice their opinions and socialise knowledge, and action commitments may become standardised into a format. A structuring element is thus introduced into the knowledge generated at the meetings, although the planning dynamics will basically continue to be unstructured, as it will focus on current problems generally emerging in everyday work.

We are now getting closer to what is known as *double loop* learning processes, that focus on innovating in the existing situation. Different conceptual approximations, experiences, objectives and available means shared by the group are compared and evaluated, in order to reach a new knowledge base or reference. Normative assumptions are questioned and analysed and even established objectives are open for discussion (Weggeman, 1997).

The problem with double loop learning is that learning processes are generally conservative and tend to confirm existing frames of reference, apart from the fact that they are a continuation of accepted knowledge. Double loop processes are not readily accepted by workers, who normally require some external motivation to enter that phase (Ibidem). External motivation may come from market dynamics and especially from external audits by clients, as has been the case in sugar mills.

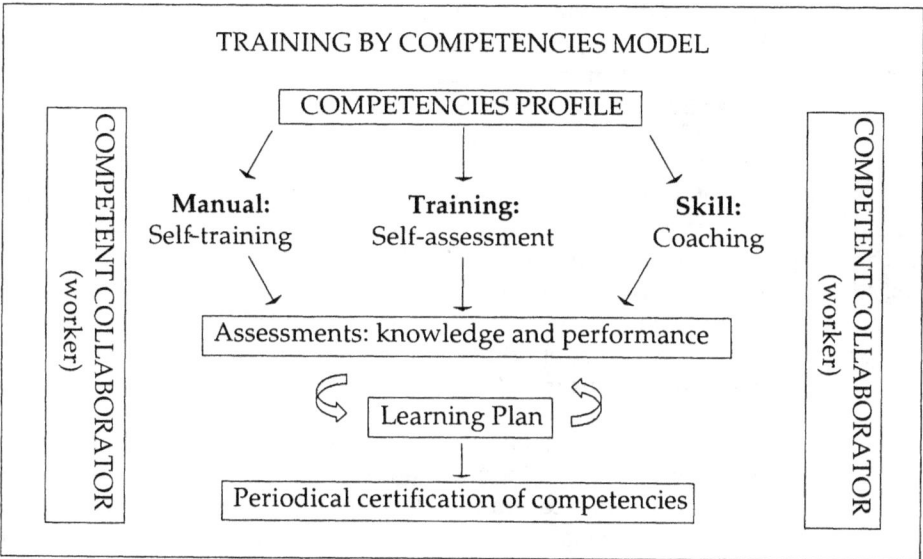

TRAINING BY COMPETENCIES MODEL

COMPETENCIES PROFILE

COMPETENT COLLABORATOR (worker)

Manual: Self-training **Training:** Self-assessment **Skill:** Coaching

Assessments: knowledge and performance

Learning Plan

Periodical certification of competencies

COMPETENT COLLABORATOR (worker)

b. Self-training and assessment guides by competencies

1. *The training by competencies model*

Self-training and assessment guides by competencies are based on the following model that comprises identification of the competencies and skills profile, training strategy, assessment of knowledge and performance, and certification.

It starts by identifying a competencies' profile or standard. Profiles can be more or less elaborated. For the garment industry in the Dominican Republic and Mexico a straightforward profile including general qualifications (providing customer satisfaction, safety at work, contributing to gender equality) and specific skills (attaching trouser hip pocket) was worked out. For sugar mills we developed a whole functional map, with competency units and elements, using a standardisation scheme of the performance and knowledge required by the function.

Irrespective of the degree of detail of a profile, the way in which it is built is the most important aspect. For profiles to reflect the strategy of organisations (what they are currently doing and what they intend to do in the future) and existing good practices, it is advisable that they should be jointly devised by high management, middle managers, technicians and some expert workers. This will help to secure the necessary support for implementation within the organisations themselves; the more persons involved, the better.

The involvement of technical groups of middle managers and expert workers has proved effective in developing profiles. The results depend to a good extent on the group dynamics technique. We recommend beginning in a holistic way, identifying the company's objectives and area as well as it strengths and weaknesses. This exercise will yield the competencies (qualifications) connected with the objectives and dysfunctions that the company will have to address. The following step is to trickle them down and specify them through tasks' analysis. This path avoids starting by individual tasks in each work post, which subsequently hinders aligning tasks with strategic objectives. It also precludes evolving a profile for each work post, which would be useless in practice for training purposes.

Group techniques vary. *Amod* ("a model", technique derived from *Dacum* – curriculum development-) focuses on "brainstorming" participants to establish the main performance procedures, that are then ordered in a curriculum or learning path: where to begin and what follows (Mertens, 2000). A profile is subsequently developed on the basis of such critical performances. Groups can also work directly on the respective profile formats and standards. When descriptions of processes are available – for example in organisations with ISO quality systems – we recommend beginning by reviewing such standards to take advantage of what the company already has.

COMPETENCIES PROFILE – SUGAR REFINERY		
Main purpose: producing increasing amounts of good-quality sugar at low cost and in environmentally favourable conditions	1. Operating equipment/ machinery	1.1 Operating equipment
		1.2 Controlling process
	2. Maintaining equipment/ area	2.1 Supporting maintenance
		2.2 Keeping area clean and orderly
	3. Lubricating equipment/ machinery	3.1 Lubricating mechanisms
		3.2 Maintaining levels
	4. Interpreting measurement parameters	4.1 Pressure gauges
		4.2 Speed gauges
		4.3 Rotameters
		4.4 Thermometers
	5. Complying with health and safety specifications	5.1 Utilising safety equipment
		5.2 Operating equipment in accordance with safety standards
	6. Working by objectives and developing improvements	6.1 Working by objectives
		6.2 Proposing improve-ments
	7. Contributing to teamwork	7.1 Keeping good communication
		7.2 Helping to solve problems
	8. Welding parts and components (optional)	8.1. Doing electric welding
		8.2 Doing autogenous welding

The time it takes to evolve a profile varies, depending on the degree of detail required for the standardisation process. In the case of the garment industry, we worked out the profile in two hours. For a food industry, we developed profiles in two stages: the first one for preparing a draft version (which took three eight-hour days) and the second one for corrections and adjustments (which took the technical team another day's work). In this instance the resulting profiles pro-

vided a much more detailed and accurate reference than in the garment industry. The objectives and contexts of the organisations account for the differences
in drawing up profiles.

The profile that we developed for sugar mills embodies an in-depth dimension of the learning process. The competencies *operating* and *maintaining* equipment broadly envisage what workers must be able to do in every department for
the refinery to work and meet its specified objectives. Knowing how to operate
and maintain comprises two key sub-competencies that are applicable in all areas: knowing how to measure and to lubricate. These are included in the profile
and add depth to its architecture. They are more easily transferable to other
branches of economic activity than the skills of operating equipment in mills.
Knowing how to measure and lubricate are qualifications required in many industrial processes, whereas operating a steam turbine or a *pachiquil* (juice separa-
tor) are more specific to sugar mills.

Another possible architecture consists of the focalised projection of the
organisation's strategy onto the profile. For example, taking the structure of the
organisation's or area's *balanced scorecard* ("balanced strategic map") and turning
it into competencies. In the case of the food industry mentioned before, the supervisors' competencies' profile to a large extent reflects a *balanced scorecard* of
the area, as it includes: final objectives (results, in quality and quantity), technological and administrative processes for reaching final objectives, development
of qualifications and technologies as dynamic support of objectives.

The dilemma concerning profile architecture is not merely a question of
greater or lesser detail. It has more complex underpinnings that are not often
investigated, overlooking an opportunity for relating competencies to productivity from the very start. To continue with the above examples, a profile's dimensions can be categorised as follows:

In the simplest category profiles can be described as one-dimensional, when
all competencies are of the same level. Bi-dimensional profiles have generic and
specific competencies; generic or in-depth competencies, or else competencies
reflecting a balanced scorecard. A three-dimensional architecture combines generic qualifications with specific and in-depth ones; or else, competencies reflecting a balanced scorecard in combination with generic, specific and in-depth qualifications. This last arrangement is not easy to be found as it implies a high level of
complexity. It would be difficult for organisations to convey a three dimensional
profile to their workers in a clear and consistent way.

Profiles are developed in detail from a previously defined format (Format 1)
that in the occupational competencies terminology is known as "standard". At

sugar mills we worked with the format used by the Mexican Conocer (Spanish acronym of the Council for the Standardisation and Certification of Occupational Competencies) that consists of the following categories: performance criteria; evidence by product and performance; evidence of knowledge; field of application by class and category; attitudes and evaluation instruments.

Format 1: Competency..........	
Performance criteria	Evidence by performance
— — — — —	— — — — —
Field of application	Evidence of knowledge
— — — — —	— — — — —
Attitudes	Evaluation instruments
— — — — —	— — — — —

In practice, this model has turned out to be laborious and not easy to build. For adequate implementation, it requires great efforts of abstraction by the team developing the standard, which are not necessarily useful for subsequent stages of the process.

A simpler and more practical model includes only the categories describing performance and evidence of knowledge (Format 2). In the course of the process, this format can be supplemented with the categories considered in the first one, if organisations think it necessary to standardise competencies more precisely. Application of this format has made it possible to channel the organisations' energy much more directly in the development of training and evaluation instruments.

Format 2: Competency.....	
Performance descriptors	Evidence of knowledge
— — — — —	— — — — —

The experience of organisations in Great Britain, where application of competencies' models is more developed, goes in the same direction. "Perhaps the most important thing learned from the experience of organisations is that this stage of the design should be short, focalised and not too ambitious. It is still common practice to take eighteen months to two years in designing a profile" (Rankin, 2001).

A format based on performance levels has been used for jobs depending to a large extent on attitudes and empirically learned skills (for instance, salesmen) (Format 3). Levels are as follows: what must not be done (basic performance of the job or function); standard performance (the sort of performance most workers can attain); outstanding performance (only attained by a few workers), and evidence of knowledge.

Format 3: Competency....	
Standard performance	Outstanding performances — — — — —
	Evidence of knowledge — — — — —
	What must not be done — — — — —

This classification was done with a twofold purpose. The first purpose was pragmatic. An evaluation of attitudes calls for accuracy in the description of expected behaviours in order to avoid ambivalence. Nonetheless, as opposed to technical qualifications, the required attitudes are not always easy to describe. The ones that are definitely not wanted are clearer, as they totally contradict the organisation's objectives and values. That is the reason why international enterprises started to include undesirable indicators in their competencies' profiles (Rankin, 2001).

The second purpose was to focalise the learning plan for each worker. If they have shown negative performances (what must not be done) they are recommended to start by the basics. After that, the next step is for them to master standard competencies. Finally, they are encouraged to aim at outstanding performances covering the whole learning path.

A point to be elucidated for bi-dimensional profiles – generic and specific qualifications – is how to deal with areas in which the two "overlap". Let us take, for example, the competency "complying with safety standards". It has a generic dimension and a specific one. In the case of sugar mills, the competencies for operating equipment and machinery comprised specific safety aspects, while the more general aspects were included in the generic competency called "working under safety standards".

Something similar occurs in sugar mills profiles of competencies relating to maintaining quality and communication, and with in-depth qualifications like knowing how to measure and lubricate, that "overlap" with the competency of operating and maintaining equipment and machinery.

We recommend involving high management in the profile-building process in order to precisely establish the project's objectives and identify essential aspects that profiles must include in the strategic view of the organisational pinnacle. Besides, high management has to be committed to supplying the necessary resources for supporting the project. Once the profile has been developed by the technical team, it is submitted to high management for validation and prosecution of its subsequent stages.

Profiles are the reference for structuring and giving consistent contents to the following instruments:

·   *Self-training manual with contents related to performance.* Contents are derived from practice and centre on critical aspects, in order to focalise the training effort and follow up generated and desired impacts.

·   *Performance self-assessment guide, that is the basis for practical training.* This guide also concentrates on critical aspects and is not just a checklist to verify what is already known in the organisation. It is a reference guiding workers along their learning path, specially for generic competencies.

·   *Development of specialisation.* Coaching by a skilled operative, supervisor or technician is carried out with the help of the manual and the self-assessment guide, so that workers may specialise in their job or function. For example, in the case of the garment industry, the jeans assembly line was grouped into six clusters of key operations. Each cluster represented an operation with varying degrees of specialisation. The manual and self-assessment guide explain all critical aspects for each specialised skill. However, without the coaching of a master operative or supervisor workers can hardly acquire the specialisation, as it requires a high proportion of tacit knowledge.

This stage consists of laying down the strategy of training based on occupational competencies or qualifications. In the particular case of sugar mills, training by competencies meant meeting at least four conditions: 1) approaching training from the critical problems existing in the factory (a problem may be critical because it is very important in the process and/or workers find it difficult to master); 2) promoting the development of abilities workers have shown in practice; 3) transferring training from the classroom to the workplace, by making workers master competency standards; 4) encouraging workers to take over their own training through the self-assessment of their technical and social abilities, which in turn promotes the creation of informal training environments.

ASSESSMENT

Take a tour of your work area with the evaluator. He will ask you to show him what is explained below. The evaluator will take down the scores and make the necessary comments to help you improve your performance.

	Knows	Does not know
Mention four pieces of personal protection equipment you must use in the plant.		
Indicate when or in what circumstances you must use safety equipment and what protection it affords.		
Show that you know how to use that equipment, placing it in the part of your body where you need it.		
Give some examples of the possible injuries or accidents you may suffer for not using the equipment.		
Show that you keep your personal protection equipment in good condition.		
To whom must you report problems with your personal protection equipment?		
How have you promoted the use of personal safety equipment among your colleagues? How can you prove it?		

25/10/2002   Ingenio Santos ILO/CIMO

The next step in the model is the evaluation of knowledge and performances. The fact that each worker keeps his own "evidence" file is what makes the difference with traditional evaluation. Instead of all responsibility devolving upon the evaluator, the evidence record turns the worker into leading player in the process. This makes it more feasible in practice for middle managers to take on the role of facilitators and evaluators of the competencies of workers in their charge.

ASSESSMENT

The evaluator will oversee you at your workplace and will ask you to show the performance of a number of operations. He will also ask you the questions included here, that you must answer.

The evaluator will grade your demonstrations and answers in a scale from 1 to 5:

1. **Beginner:** does not know how to perform or answer
2. **In training:** can answer and perform up to a point, but needs support to reach standard.
3. **Standard:** can answer and perform the required minimum, but needs support to solve unforeseen situations.
4. **In development:** can perform and answer fully and solve unforeseen and difficult situations.
5. **Professional:** has developed fully and can teach other persons.

At the end of every section there is a space for the evaluator to include his comments, which will guide you in all aspects of your future development. You are also asked to sign your conformity with the results of the evaluation.

Organisations generally keep their middle managers busy in a variety of tasks and functions. Assigning to them the additional role of facilitators/evaluators will only be in order if the administrative aspects of the process do not take up too much of their time. For the technical part of explaining contents, facilitators can rely on expert workers to help out colleagues requiring special support. Facilitation thus becomes a shared function rather than the sole responsibility of middle managers.

Knowledge assessment is based on compliance with the instructions of self-training guides. The instructions and exercises provide guidance for study of the manual. Trainees will find the answers further on in the manual, and can look them up when they perform requested exercises. The degree of difficulty found in the guides will depend on the schooling and education of workers and on the level of responsibility assigned to them in their job.

Performance assessment is done with a checklist of observations and outcomes. Workers' individual self-assessments are taken into account insofar as they fit in.

Evaluators are generally supervisors but they can also be master workers or specialists. In assessing both knowledge and performance they have the support of a verifier or referee, a person from outside but well versed in the competency.

The scale of application of assessments is a point for debate. Some maintain that competencies can only be judged in two ways: workers are either competent or incompetent. That was the criterion adopted in sugar mills.

Evaluating in this manner has several disadvantages. Firsly, it is not always evident that workers are competent or otherwise in their performance. Secondly, both workers and organisations are interested in knowing how near (or far) they are from expected standards, for reasons of motivation and the resources that will have to be devoted to achieving competency. Thirdly, it is also useful to know in what competencies workers rise above expected standards, for that can constitute a resource for training other workers or balance out the process according to individual abilities. For all those reasons, in the garment and food industries mentioned before we opted for a scale of more points (5 and 4, respectively).

LEARNING ACTION PLAN				
Competencies to develop	Action to engage in	Support needs	Deadline	Action undertaken

Signature of worker ——————— Signature supervisor ————————

Signature verifier ———————————

The results of assessments provide the terms of reference for learning plans. For example, in the garment industry we opted for two assessments a year. After each assessment, workers and evaluators established individual learning plans, in accordance with the needs unveiled by the assessment and the organisation's priorities. During the period preceding the next assessment, workers provide evidence that they are complying with the learning plan, using such evidence as the main input for the subsequent assessment.

For the garment industry in the Dominican Republic and the transport workers of the food company in Mexico we decided to certify personnel once a year. When certification took place each year, workers had to show that they were able to keep up their competency. The certifications' content may vary from one year to another as instruments are refined and new items are incorporated or prioritised by the company.

In sugar mills, workers give proof of their competency at the end of the assessment process by complying with established criteria. Subsequent assessments refer to other competencies or qualifications. Only when there are significant changes in technology, in the organisation or its priorities, are workers evaluated anew for competencies that had already been assessed.

In the occupational competencies' model instructors and supervisors also play the role of facilitators and evaluators. To achieve consistency and quality in the application of the various instruments, facilitators should be previously trained as facilitators/evaluators. This trainers' training focuses on understanding and implementing the manual of procedures for application of training/assessment instruments. In addition, it is a training that balances formal and informal aspects and is effected through classroom induction, coaching and follow-up in practice.

In the case of the food company we specifically developed a manual for the training of facilitators/evaluators. In designing it we followed the established principles of training by competencies' manuals. Its contents are not confined to procedures but refer to concepts relating to training by competencies and explain how to apply instruments. It also includes a competency profile of facilitators/evaluators and verifiers which enables to evaluate facilitators/evaluators and internal verifiers further on in the process with a view to ensuring overall quality.

Certification may be internal or external. The food company opted for internal certification. In the clothes-making industries of the Dominican Republic certification is conducted externally by the National TVET Institute (Infotep).

GENERAL ASSESSMENT /CERTIFICATION PROCEDURE (sugar mills)

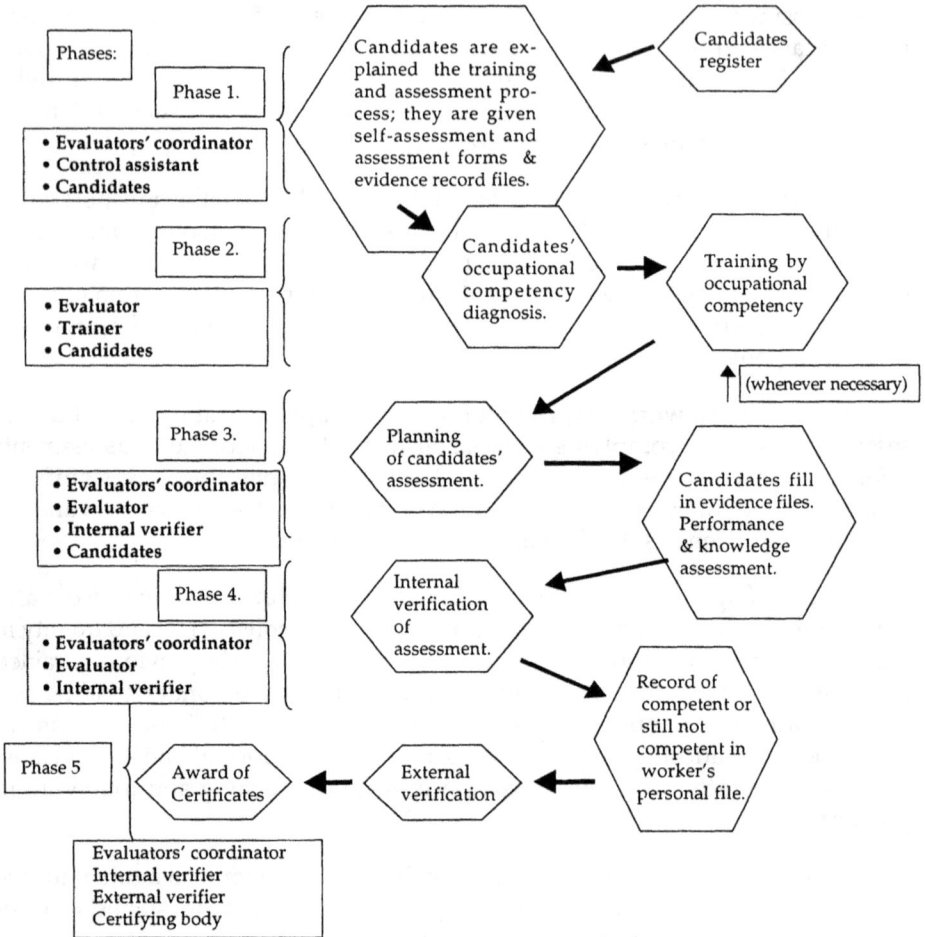

Phases:

Phase 1.
- Evaluators' coordinator
- Control assistant
- Candidates

Phase 2.
- Evaluator
- Trainer
- Candidates

Phase 3.
- Evaluators' coordinator
- Evaluator
- Internal verifier
- Candidates

Phase 4.
- Evaluators' coordinator
- Evaluator
- Internal verifier

Phase 5
Evaluators' coordinator
Internal verifier
External verifier
Certifying body

Candidates are explained the training and assessment process; they are given self-assessment and assessment forms & evidence record files.

Candidates register

Candidates' occupational competency diagnosis.

Training by occupational competency

(whenever necessary)

Planning of candidates' assessment.

Candidates fill in evidence files. Performance & knowledge assessment.

Internal verification of assessment.

Record of competent or still not competent in worker's personal file.

Award of Certificates

External verification

In the case of sugar mills, certification is also external through a certifying body created as part of the National System of Competencies promoted by *Conocer* in Mexico. Sugar mills have been accredited as evaluation centres by the external certification body. A fundamental aspect of this accreditation is the preparation of a manual of procedures of the assessment and internal verification processes. Once the manual has been issued, evidence must be provided that evaluators and internal verifiers are trained to apply it. After some experience, they have in turn to assess and certify themselves as evaluators and internal verifiers.

Benefits identified for the whole organisation as a result of application of a competencies' model in personnel selection and development:

· *Personnel happier in the exercise of their duties.*
· *Improved productivity, as operatives have the basic competencies for adequate performance of their function.*
· *Higher performance standards.*
· *Better service to customers, as employees can interact more effectively and efficiently with them.*
· *Lower personnel turnover.*
· *Workers feel motivated and responsible for developing their abilities and knowledge, using competencies' profiles to identify areas of opportunity in their individual careers plan.*

(Parker, 2001)

It is up to the organisation – sugar mill in this case – to maintain its accreditation as evaluation centre, by following the observations of external audits made by the certifying body, and taking the necessary corrective action.

After these steps, how is the cycle closed by improved productivity and working conditions? There is no mechanism directly ensuring a contribution to enhanced productivity and working conditions. It is difficult to isolate the impact of learning through the above mentioned instruments, or through other determining factors such as technology and organisation.

However, it is possible to relate learning efforts to enhancement of productivity and working conditions, in an indirect manner. The simplest way is a longitudinal comparison of some key productivity and working conditions indicators within a given area. Rather more complicated are comparisons with control groups to which the instruments have not been applied.

In both cases, readings are not linear or direct. Analysis starts in the surrounding environment to isolate external factors affecting the results. Once they have been identified and their impact has been evaluated, comparisons can be made over time or between groups.

A decline of the indicators does not necessarily mean that the learning effort has been in vain but it is a warning for reviewing its effectiveness. Inversely, an improvement of the indicators does not necessarily result from application of the learning instruments, but is a sign that the process is yielding positive results.

In a pilot project with a group of salesmen of the food company, we related performance assessment by competencies with productivity results in a given area, both longitudinally within that area and comparatively with a control group. Over a six month period we achieved sufficiently impressive results for the company's management to decide to extend the project to other areas.

This does not mean that all results were higher than those of the control group. Even if all indicators had shown better results than those of the control group, that would not have necessarily convinced the company's directors. Experts know that results depend on many factors, and there are ways of boosting them in the short term (for instance, a sales promotion campaign).

What persuaded directors was the consistency of the model and the objective explanation of results by facilitators, showing the pros and cons of the experience. Enterprises do not expect spectacular results, for they know they can vanish as quickly as they came up. What they do want are sound and consistent proposals showing positive results, both in quality and quantity in favourable and unfavourable situations; proposals that are likely to last, and not just meaningless routines from the point of view of learning and ongoing improvement.

TRAINING AND ASSESSMENT GUIDE

Your name:

Date of delivery of guide:

Dates of assessments:

UNIT 5: COMPLYING WITH STANDARDS OF HEALTH AND SAFETY AT WORK

The objective of this training and assessment guide is that you apply and follow standards of health and safety at work.

How to use the guide:

1. You must read it carefully.
2. You must fill in the **self-assessment** spaces, that is to say, you yourself must indicate what you can and cannot do, what you know and do not know.
3. Once you have finished your self-assessment, go to your chief and review it with him, to see what you lack for being considered a COMPETENT WORKER.

17/09/2002   Ingenios Santos / ILO / CIMO

Building Self-training Guides (Manuals)

Self-training guides are the basic learning element of the proposed model. In some cases, when attitudes and behaviour patterns are essential for performance (*eg.* salesmen), performance evaluation instruments have played that role. However, this does not detract from the importance of performance assessment instruments. It stems rather from the tradition of how training is delivered in organisations. Workers and organisations themselves feel safer and more comfortable when performance assessment is accompanied by a tangible instrument with explicit knowledge, like a manual.

However, not just any manual is acceptable and organisations have become more demanding about the cost-benefit relation of training manuals. They question their usefulness, specially when workers have a low level of formal training or their job consists of simple and repetitive tasks. They want manuals not to deviate from concrete work situations and at all moments respond to the changing learning needs of workers and enterprises. The other side of such expected benefits is the cost incurred.

The cost of learning instruments is a key aspect for organisations nowadays, a costly instrument in design and/or application will come up against objections from the very beginning and will be out of line with the sign of the times for organisations. This does not mean that organisations are opposed to investing in learning instruments, but they expect the investment to decrease in relation to the learning activities undertaken. According to this rationale, the amounts invested may grow in time depending on the results obtained, providing learning outcomes are proportionally more fruitful. How can this be achieved? By ensuring that organisations make instruments and procedures their own, part of their daily working routine. This is the challenge faced by training by competencies projects like the one we are submitting.

In view of these demands and requirements by organisations, we devised a self-study guide where contents are derived from concrete work, reflecting normal situations and contingencies. Visual references are connected with real and recognisable working conditions. They thus contribute to generate a safe and reliable atmosphere, which helps workers to assimilate and adopt the guide, preventing them from seeing it as an instrument removed from their everyday functions.

The self-training guide is an instrument with structured contents, to be applied informally in diverse situations and not just in the classroom.[14] The instruc-

---

14 We are referring to the printed guide. It was also turned into an interactive multimedia instrument where both versions (CD and printed guide) complemented each other.

tor need not be one single person; the learning process may be helped along by different people and/or facilitators that are not always recognised beforehand as such. Informality implies that neither the place nor the form or persons taking part are predetermined. It is not reflected in the contents of the learning process but rather in its application, which includes various modes of self-study.

Guides are based on the context in which subject contents are applied. They intend to stimulate learners by contextualising contents, and combining different (self)assessment techniques that lead candidates step by step in their learning, alternating reflection with practice and related technical aspects.

Guides may be used in groups or individually, with the help of a facilitator or instructor, that varies in each case. After finishing their self-assessment, learners (workers) ask the evaluator to assess them.

The contents of guides are predefined as well as the situations in which they are applied. However, the assessment process may include non-coded contents when evaluators interact with candidates beyond the evaluation format. The purpose is then to turn evaluation into an open-ended training process.

The object of assessment is the knowledge associated to performance. In the case of the sugar mills and the garment industry each module of the manual ends with an evaluation guide that integrates knowledge and performances into a single instrument. In the food enterprise we opted for separating knowledge from performance evaluations. The knowledge assessment instrument refers to the quality of the response generated by each module in self-assessing. The performance assessment instrument is a checklist of observations and products. The checklist envisages first a self-assessment followed by an assessment.

Development of manuals is a construction process comprising the selection of contents, self-assessment techniques and decisions about the degree of depth and detail intended.

The main steps of manual building are as follows:

Once the profile of key competencies and their respective sub-competencies have been established, the SCID format is applied to the latter (SCID, Systematic Curriculum Instructional Development) (Mertens, 1997c).

MAKING REAR PIPING* CORRECTLY

Show the following to the evaluator, or answer his questions about it. Depending on the results, the evaluator will give you a score in the box, according to the scale.

Describe the steps you take to make the piping,
show how safety is ensured
in the operation and how the pieces are ordered in sequence.

Show how you use machines and tools carefully.

Show the needles you use for the operation.

Show that you know how to thread, change needles and
put bobbins in place.

Show that you keep your working area and machine clean and
always place a cloth under it, even during recesses.

What unforeseen situations can occur, and how do you solve them?

What are the typical errors, and their consequences?

Show how you protect yourself during this operation (safety).
What is the evidence that you always do so?

What do you report, and to whom? What is the evidence?

What negative attitude must you avoid?
　　　What is the evidence that you actually avoid it?

What positive attitude must you show?
　　　What is the evidence that you actually show it?

Action plan and commitment:

Average score

Worker's signature　　Evaluator's signature　　Verifier's signature　　Date:

* Piping: ornamental trimming on clothes' seams (jeans in this case)

This first step is a coding or illustration of the knowledge applied in connection with the competency in question, consisting of the performance of routines, solving of typical contingencies, related knowledge, safety aspects and attitudes, as well as "negative" indicators (what must be avoided or not done). It includes some open, uncoded spaces for the tacit elements of competencies. The depth is contemplated in the design of the exercises that have to reflect the complexity of the job and refer to real work situations based on the analysis of "expert" workers, supervisors and directors.

I. SELF-ASSESSMENT

CLIENT SATISFACTION

- WHO ARE OUR CUSTOMERS?

- WHAT DO OUR CUSTOMERS EXPECT?

- WHICH ARE THE MOST COMMON ERRORS WE MAKE THAT AFFECT QUALITY?

- WHAT MUST WE DO WHEN WE DETECT A QUALITY PROBLEM?

25/10/2002 infotep-IP

At this stage it is important to establish which are the critical contents to prevent the guides from becoming operational manuals (information about operations) instead of learning instruments (transforming information into understanding). Focusing on certain critical aspects makes it possible to steer the instruments towards their specific impact. It also brings down the cost of developing and applying them, and marks out the efforts to be made both by workers and evaluators in their implementation.

A second important aspect is the balance between the knowledge already existing in the organisation, based on its good practices, and the new knowledge coming from the environment and the path the organisation wishes to follow in the immediate future. External knowledge may also be incorporated owing to the need to deepen existing know-how.

GUIDING CRITERIA FOR DEVELOPING SELF-TRAINING MATERIAL

Contents' dimensions

1. Describing the expected behaviour standard in relation to the subject dealt with.
2. Establishing basic functions and principles (routines, procedures) in a real work context.
3. Developing subject on the basis of critical aspects in a real work context.

Development

4. Establishing modular structure according to the competencies defined.
5. Referring to the problems that crop up in work in connection with the subject in question.
6. Explaining *whys and wherefores* on the basis of examples, using graphic material and images.
7. Describing and explaining what happens if the operation is not done, or the procedure is not followed correctly.
8. Including exercises (real situations, simulations, theory) and games.

Assessment

9. Formulating self-assessment schemes.
10. Describing aspects and conditions of personnel assessment.

Principles

The teaching material is just an approximation to expected performances. It will only make reference to critical aspects. The link between the two will be established in practice.
This must not become an operational manual.

Selection criteria become apparent here once again, as we are not trying to produce a replica of a book on engineering or human behaviour in teamwork, but to explain enough for workers to understand why some actions have to be carried out and how. We will only go into more complex and/or deeper levels of understanding when necessary.

A third aspect is the placing of contents within a given context. We cannot start by explaining specific technical or social aspects. What organisations want nowadays is that their operational personnel should be aware of the *reasons* for their job and tasks. That they should be acquainted with, the objectives and priorities of their own area and organisation, and know how to contribute to such objectives from their microspace in the enterprise.

One of the overall objectives that many organisations pursue is client satisfaction. What must every worker show or prove? How is a contribution to client satisfaction made evident? (internal or external customers) How does it generate added value for clients? The answers to these queries and proof that they are being met are requirements of the latest version of ISO quality systems.

Including this point in the initial part of each sub-competency has a twofold purpose. In the first place, it brings the sub-competency into line with objectives and priorities, which is in turn a selection mechanism as it is difficult to specify its contribution to the objectives and its inclusion in the manual has to be analysed more carefully. Secondly, it makes workers and facilitators aware that the sum of particularities does not necessarily lead to the objectives, unless each one of them has incorporated them basically in their development.

The second stage is the preparation of the training guides. In our first experiences we began to ask ourselves what were the characteristics of a manual or teaching guide by competencies. We had the intuition that most of the manuals that organisations were using to train their personnel had not been designed with a competencies' approach. Nevertheless, it was not so clear why this was so and no criteria had been defined that manuals had to comply with to be based on competencies.

In order to be consistent, we have chosen some criteria based on the literature and experiences that we recommend following in the drafting of manuals. This is not an exhaustive or definitive checklist but a proposal open to improvements. These criteria help positioning manuals by competencies *vis-à-vis* traditional ones. They also make it possible to visualise and understand the modifications and improvements incorporated into the model in the course of time. Consequently, they constitute a reference for managing institutional learning about training by competencies.

USING PERSONAL SAFETY EQUIPMENT

- **You are competent when:**

➢ You use your safety equipment;

➢ You keep your safety equipment in good condition;

➢ You promote the use of safety equipment among your colleagues;

➢ You know how to utilise the factory's industrial safety equipment;

➢ You explain the protection afforded by each personal safety item;

➢ You explain to others the protection that the personal safety equipment gives you;

➢ You explain to others the visual safety signs in your working area.

25/10/2002 Ingenio Santos / ILO / CIMO

A typical course for the preparation of manuals is the following:

1. As title for the module we can take the name of the qualification, for example, in the case of sugar mills, "Using the personal safety equipment".

2. We specify the performances and knowledge workers must show to qualify for the competency. For instance: "Keeping your safety equipment in good condition". If there are different performances and/or evidences of knowledge, or if we want to go deeper into one of them, we can opt for several sub-modules.

3. We continue by developing the self-evaluation section. Here we can use various knowledge assessment techniques like, for example, open-ended questions, multiple choice problems, associations, hits and misses in images, crossword puzzles, completion of sentences, etc.

    The ideal solution is to mix several techniques to prevent tiredness, but we can opt for a routine of questions that are repeated for each competency. We did so for the garment industry and it enabled us to make much faster progress in building our manuals. In the Dominican Republic, using that scheme we developed two manuals for two different enterprises in two weeks' time.

Contents include two kinds of knowledge: a) knowledge directly associated with a given performance: *eg.* what must I do to keep my personal safety equipment in good condition?, what must I do when steam pressure exceeds the allowed limit? (such knowledge enables workers to understand the expected behaviour); b) knowledge aimed at developing cognitive abilities, and referring to the principles of phenomena, and cause-effect relations, *eg.* explaining the risks of steam pressure exceeding upper limits.

A just balance will have to be struck between these two areas of knowledge in the construction of manuals. This applies to the four key moments of learning in a labour context: a) routines and procedures in "normal" operation conditions; b) action required of workers in unusual or contingency situations; c) typical errors to be avoided; d) improvements workers may suggest about procedures, processes, human relations, working conditions and the manuals themselves.

SELF-ASSESSMENT

Give some examples of safety equipment in bad condition.

_____

_____

Belt.: _____

| Point out what you do to keep your safety equipment in good condition | → |

Apron.: _____

Goggles.: _____

Boots.: _____

↓

Gloves.: _____   Helmet.: _____   Raincoat.: _____   Mask.: _____

TO WHOM DO YOU REPORT YOUR PROBLEMS WITH YOUR PERSONAL SAFETY EQUIPMENT?

Indicate with XX to whom you **must necessarily** report.

Indicate with X to whom **it is advisable** to report.

CMU   Head of Industrial relations.   Field director.

Head of another department.   Shift leader.   Head of laboratory.

Equipment manager.   ProMES Board.   Head of procurement.

25/10/2002 Ingenio Santos / ILO / CIMO

This last point opens up new vistas for organisational knowledge. It is important that employees know not only what their organisation expects them to know, but also what its dysfunctions or opportunities may reveal from a productive point of view or reality. Direct operation of the process and concrete experiences in it are constantly generating new knowledge in workers. For such knowledge to turn into organisational learning and know-how, socialisation and reflection mechanisms are required. Manuals provide one such mechanism by including spaces for critical reflection.

4. In the technical information section workers will find explanations of the subjects dealt with in the self-assessment section. Answers are included there to many of the questions and exercises posed in the self-evaluation. This is part of a self-information strategy. Whenever they require, workers may check whether they have understood the topic and answered questions correctly. Sometimes there is more than one answer to the same question, depending on the underlying technology and organisation.

TECHNICAL EXPLANATION

To whom do you report problems with your personal safety equipment?

XX. To whom you must **necessarily** report	X. To whom it is **advisable** to report.
CMU **XX**	Head of Industrial relations **X**
Field Director	Head of another department..
Shift leader **XX**	Head of laboratory
Equipment manager.	ProMES Board **X**
	Head of procurement **X**

17/09/2002 Ingenio Santos / ILO /CIMO

81

The proposed link between self-assessment and technical explanation is based on the following assumptions:

- The challenge of answering questions and doing exercises connected with their job motivates workers.
- The relationship established enables workers to use the manual at their own rate and when they do not necessarily have the support of a facilitator.
- The visual presentation of the material and the answers and exercises provided in the technical explanation, act as references and examples that make the manuals accessible even for persons of low schooling level.
- The modular structure with sub-modules and exercises enables trainees to keep abreast with their learning, and prevents them from despairing and losing motivation.
- The transparency of the process, that consists of answering questions and doing exercises with the answers to hand, allays the workers' fears of being in evidence for lack of knowledge. They have to rely on their own judgement, which gives leverage to their learning, provided that they consider the contents valid and attainable.
- The development of information technology, that makes it possible to access databases with drawings and graphs and to incorporate digital pictures, places these manuals within the reach of most organisations. They are flexible instruments, easily adapted to changing circumstances and/or new learning demands that may emerge.

Their modular design and self-assessment/technical explanation structure makes them liable to multi-media adaptation (*eg.* an interactive CD) or learning via *Internet or Intranet*. In the case of the food enterprise we used an interactive CD as a complement to the printed manual and group exercises.

Preparation of the technical explanations has several difficulties.

The first and perhaps most important one is the natural conflict between knowledge derived from practice and that derived from the coded science of books and other media. This conflict surfaces through persons with different hierarchical positions in the organisation. Practical knowledge is more frequent among operatives and coded scientific knowledge among technicians and directors.

A balance of the two is struck by participants in the project that come from different spheres and positions in the organisation. Project leaders should be aware of this conflict and implement effective facilitation to achieve a balanced structure.

Another frequent side effect is the following. What happens when the project leader, technician or director is changed? The newcomer's temptation to review the manual and go through the building process again may be exceedingly great. We can easily imagine he will find defects and faults, particularly because his predecessor took part in the design. If at a given moment there is no clear-cut leadership because the project has been assimilated or taken over by the organisation, the problem is how to maintain the balance with the new authorities. Many projects have come to a complete halt for that reason, at least for a while.

The attitudes and emotional intelligence to be developed in middle and upper managers are circumscribed to competencies:

- Motivating and inspiring collaborators, by establishing goals and setting a direction.
- Making conscious and effective efforts in support of workers' development towards significantly better performances.
- Communicating with a clear vision of collaborators.
- Identifying, facing and solving problems that come up in the group of collaborators.
- Being prepared to learn from collaborators.
- Taking collaborators' concerns as one's own and conveying them to upper management.
- Whenever necessary, breaking unpleasant news to workers but keeping their performance at desired levels.
- Scrutinising assumptions, procedures, processes and generating imaginative, innovative, creative and practical concepts to solve problems.
- Showing enthusiasm and commitment to tasks.
- Identifying the strengths of collaborators, and delegating tasks and responsibilities to them.
- Periodically reviewing the individual performance of collaborators and providing feedback to them.
- Consulting with workers for decision making, and involving them in the process.
- Learning about the feelings of collaborators and supporting them emotionally if necessary.
- Controlling anger, disappointment and despair; keeping calm and maintaining a respectful relationship with collaborators.

Competency, various issues. IRS, London, 2000-2002

The problem of balancing the two types of knowledge has complex underpinnings and cannot be solved only with an instrumental approach. It requires a process of social analysis and interaction to modify attitudes and develop the emotional intelligence of middle and upper managers.

They are seldom inclined to listen to workers and collaborators and accept their knowledge as valid. The same as in the ProMES model, in order to be successful this proposal for guides requires that middle and upper managers should understand the meaning of the process and accept their role in it. But above all, they should acquire different attitudinal and emotional competencies from those of traditional management.

Traditionally, middle and upper managers of organisations in Latin America have considered that leadership means "having the last word", and have imposed their will in an authoritarian fashion. They frequently confuse their commanding position with the attributes of a social ruling class and underestimate their subordinates or deal with them in a paternalistic way. Such attitudes do not favour the creation of a learning atmosphere, whatever the instrument or techniques applied.

The *second* problem is the degree of depth with which each subject is considered. The criterion followed is that work needs will dictate how deep we must go. In fact, this occurs in practice because progress is made in the construction of the manual when participants make a selection demarcating depth, according to how they imagine the material in hand may be of use to workers.

INTEGRATION PRINCIPLES OF MANUALS

- Examples
- Conducted and open-ended exercises
- Ludic (games)
- Graphic
- Real imagery, recognisable and familiar situations
- Use of well known locutions or popular philosophy language
- Alternation of typefaces and colours
- Constantly changing feelings and associations in presentations (surprise element)

Despite curricula are derived from practice, we must be aware of the fact that practical views are subjective and topics might be considered in depth not necessarily because practice requires so, but because the organisation's technician that is in charge masters a particular topic. A way of counteracting such deviations is requesting a review of the material by several of the organisation's technicians and directors and, if possible, asking for the opinion of outside experts. Another method – not the only one- is following up the application of the manuals and asking learners and evaluators what areas need further elaboration. In the manual we prepared for drivers of heavy-duty vehicles of the food company we included paragraphs in each module asking workers and evaluators to say what subjects needed to be treated in more detail. After such answers are inventoried, a selection is made and a new version of the manual can be issued.

The *third* problem is to achieve creativity in the design of exercises and technical explanations. Organisations generally lack that capability. Persons charged with the drafting and preparation of manuals need to be trained in the use of knowledge evaluation techniques. The most successful method is through examples and coaching in relation to the manual they are constructing.

The most difficult thing is to unlearn the concept prevailing in organisations (sometimes unconsciously) about the way in which adults learn. The traditional scholastic path of beginning by basic principles and developing them in a se-

---

KNOWLEDGE ASSESSMENT TECHNIQUES

- **CONSTRUCTED ANSWERS:**
  - RESTRICTED ANSWERS (give two reasons why…)
  - EXTENDED ANSWERS (explain importance of service for the client…)
  - STRUCTURED QUESTIONS
    (description of a process, plus specific questions)

- **SELECTION ANSWERS:**
  - MULTIPLE CHOICES
  - MULTIPLE ANSWERS
  - ASSOCIATION-RELATIONSHIP
  - MATRIX OF ANSWERS
  - ALTERNATE ANSWERS (true or false)
  - HIT OR MISS – REASONING (true or false, and why?)

---

quential and linear manner, is not the most appropriate method for training grownups. Adults want to associate new knowledge with their concrete life experiences. Pressed for time in studying a manual, lacking reading habits and leaning towards learning by practice, workers need to find incentives in the contents and design of manuals in order not to be put off after the first couple of pages.

To support manual construction we have made a checklist of possible techniques for evaluating knowledge.

Incorporation of such techniques into manuals is based on the assumption that adults expect, on the one hand, a clear-cut structuring of subjects, which enables them to visualise their progress and, on the other hand, a similarity of the contents with the complex reality of their work experience. Work processes are far removed from linear, programmed sequences of activities. They rather resemble the simultaneous existence of different realities: what we must do according to standards, and what experience tells us; errors to avoid and what to do in contingencies; the information we must look up to make decisions; safety aspects to be observed. All these factors and several others (communication, attitudes, emotions) are present at the same time but on different planes. Routine operation will prevail at one moment, communication and decision the next.

Contents are represented on those various planes coming near to the realities of job performance. Not all of them are always present, depending on the importance ascribed to each one. A differentiated presentation of the same subject area induces learners to associate planes dynamically with their own life experiences, without feeling compelled by a linear, monotonous sequence.

The *fourth* problem is the cost of reproduction of manuals. All workers are supposed to have their own manual, where they do exercises and jot down anything they may consider important. Manuals thus turn into evidence of what workers have thought about the contents, through the quantity and quality of their answers to exercises. Manuals are also instruments that prevent knowledge from vanishing and refresh workers' memory whenever required.

Issuing a manual for each worker is not always within the possibilities or priorities of an organisation, particularly when personnel turnover is high. In the case of sugar mills, we opted for printing manuals by parts and in black and white, to bring down the cost of reproducing more than 100 pages. Copies were bulky because we used large typeface and many photos and pictures to make them easier to understand.

The issue of costs is both relative and real. Manuals of a length and quality generally meeting the expectations of workers and employers can be reproduced at costs ranging from U$S 25 and 35 per unit. The problem is that organisations consider it as a cost and not as an investment. It can indeed be a cost when the model does not generate a process of learning and improvement in the organisation. Scepticism prevails among most managers of Latin American organisations, which is quite understandable. When they buy machinery or equipment by the specifications they know what theoretically is the costs/benefit ratio, i.e. the evolution of the demand for the product or service and the expected operation of the installed equipment.

In the case of training based on manuals and the evaluation of performances, the cost/benefit relation is more difficult to establish. Firstly, because the organisation has no information about the shortcomings of each worker *vis-à-vis* the competency required by the job. Secondly, even assuming that we managed to get that information through knowledge and performance assessments, it would be difficult to calculate the impact training might have in levelling workers' competencies for productivity, owing to the influence of other factors, as already pointed out in this document. Thirdly, there may be undesired qualitative impacts in an unfavourable labour atmosphere, bad communication, human relations, that have their own weight and cannot be assessed in terms of money. Fourthly, organisations lack a culture of relating training with productive processes and productivity and both of them have been traditionally seen as separate compartments.

However, relating training to expected impact is not a senseless endeavour, therefore, we must establish what we mean by benefits. On one hand, there are tangible benefits, directly linked to the organisation's financial results (costs, sales). On the other hand, gains can be intangible, such as client satisfaction, successful teamwork, a good labour climate, the ability for reacting in contingencies and innovating; *esprit de corps*, participation and personnel enthusiasm; communication, workers' satisfaction with their job.

These intangibles may lead to very tangible effects, such as personnel stability, reduced accidents and absenteeism, better quality processes, response times, etc.

There are also institutional benefits insofar as training through manuals and performance evaluation instruments shows that organisations are meeting the demands of the market or the State. For example, ISO 9000 standards include personnel training as a requirement organisations must comply with for qualifying internationally. In the food industry, the international standard of safety and good manufacturing practices (HACCP - *Hazard Analysis Critical Control Point*) requires proof of personnel training and competence in the matter. In sectors where there are risks for the population, like motor transport, States require employees to comply with the required knowledge. In some countries (like Mexico, for example) organisations are required by law to have training plans for their personnel and to provide evidence of their training action. In others (like the Dominican Republic) they must pay a percentage of their payroll to a training fund or institution, and may get support from them when submitting a personnel training plan.

For manuals and their respective performance evaluation instruments to yield concrete results (tangible, intangible or institutional results) they have to be established before they are applied. This means guiding the process, providing feedback during implementation, evaluating it periodically and making proposals for upgrading it. It is also useful for the operational area to make the project its own, by coordinating it strategically and organically with its technological, administrative and systems' processes, so that the project will contribute almost naturally to the organisation's objectives.

4
APPLICATION AND INSTITUTIONAL LEARNING PATHWAYS: ProMES AND SELF-TRAINING AND ASSESSMENT GUIDES BY COMPETENCIES

In Latin America, during the 1995-2002 period and in the framework of ILO technical co-operation, specially through Cinterfor, the ProMES and Self-training and Assessment Guides (STAG) models were submitted to various social actors: employers' organisations, trade unions, labour ministries and technical/vocational training institutions.

The idea was not to clone a model that had been designed for other contexts, but rather to adapt its methodological outline for consistent and coherent application. This is the outcome of that effort and of the endogenous training capacity of each organisation, coordinated with institutional learning processes.

Institutional learning occurs at two levels. The first one is learning by the technical/vocational training institution itself, and the second one, learning by the organisation or enterprise. Both processes are not separate in time and contents but interact through reflection on concrete experiences, which makes the methodological proposal dynamic. It proceeds according to the learning generated and the needs that emerge along the way. Neither training institutions nor organisations are expected to take the proposal literally, but to adapt it to their own requirements, capacities and possibilities.

Apart from similar initiatives in several other nations of the region, by the year 2000 the proposal had found significant response in Mexico and the Dominican Republic. Initial applications have been recently made in Cuba but this paper concentrates on experiences in the first two countries.

In both countries the proposal was systematically received by enterprises and technical/vocational training (TVET) institutions. They started by a process of adaptation and improvement. At annual meetings of the leading players, experts of the institutions involved and Cinterfor/ILO, experiences have been systematically analysed and evaluated. Those meetings offered an opportunity for exchanging successful practices, exploring new avenues and became an instrument for guiding and promoting institutional learning according to the models put forward.

a. ProMES in Mexico

Application of ProMES started in 1995 in a medium-sized sugar mill in the State of Jalisco. In the beginning it had the support of the Overall Quality and Modernisation programme (Spanish acronym CIMO), of the Labour and Social Security Secretariat (STyPS), and the ILO. On the basis of that experience, the model was subsequently applied in other sectors and branches of the economy, like small rural producers, *maquila* export plants, service stations (gas stations). However, it was in sugar mills that application was more systematic and generated a significant process of institutional and organisational learning.

Context

When application of ProMES began at the "Bellavista" sugar mill in 1995, the Mexican macro-economic context was characterised by a deep economic crisis in the midst of an accelerated process of trade opening and State deregulation that had started more than a decade before. The more dynamic sectors had been modernised technologically and organisationally to face the structural reforms (Mertens, 1997). But many others reacted more slowly and lagged behind in adapting to the new circumstances. The sugar industry was one of those, probably the most slow-moving among manufacturing industries.[15]

This backwardness was reflected in low sugar yields and energy generation in the plants, bad and uneven quality of the sugar, underemployed personnel and high operational costs by international standards. The picture was further complicated in subsequent years, and excess production was nearly 20% a year. To this was added a drop in the international price of sugar, and the replacement of cane sugar by corn fructose in the confectionery and light beverages indus-

---

15 As compared to the Brazilian sugar industry, it lags approximately 30 years behind, according to a Brazilian expert.

tries. In 2002, the extent of that substitution in the region was of 10 to 15% of the national market early (Mertens; Wilde, 2001).

The situation was also reflected at social level. The typical profile of workers was low degree of schooling (an average of four to five years of elementary education), advanced age (average, 45 years or more), many years' seniority in the plant, and occasional attendance of a training course (many workers had never done so). Working conditions were far from decent: high accident rates, scarce use of personal safety implements, non-existent signs, proliferation of unsafe and unhealthy situations. Labour relations consisted of the confrontation of enterprise and trade union, in the frame of a rigid Contract-Law plagued with ineffectual details; bargaining centred on the interests of owners/managers and union leaders, while those of workers and the enterprise itself were relegated or totally disregarded.

The corporate culture was one of survival, with a minimum of investments and no prospects of competitiveness in the medium term. The union culture was how to take the greatest possible advantage of any changes in the established work routine, paying no heed to the survival limitations of the enterprise in the market. Both management and the trade union acted on the assumption that at any signs of liquidity or solvency problems, the Government would provide the necessary support. They were justified by the social significance of sugar mills in terms of industrial employment generation in rural areas, where labour and income options were scarce. Under this circumstances, mills had become overcrowded in previous years, when they were in the hands of the State (Ibidem).

With this structural picture in the industry and in the middle of the 1995 macro-economic crisis, a national consensus was apparent in labour circles (entrepreneurs, trade unions, labour secretariat) that the economic situation called for new employment policies. But there was also agreement that medium and long term policies should not be left aside, and aimed at training personnel in the new competencies that technological and organisational changes demanded.

As a strategy for keeping and generating jobs in the face of trade opening and State deregulation, a steady improvement of productivity and an equitable distribution of benefits among the actors involved in production were suggested.

The ILO shared this view, with the proviso that improved productivity should be a necessary but not sufficient condition for generating jobs of the required quality. With the advent of the concept of "decent work" in the late 'nineties that attitude was stressed further. Only productivity improvements would be acceptable stemming from, and leading to working conditions considered to be decent or dignified the world over.

This is clearly expressed in a text about decent work as an objective for economic and social development, that in analysing the systemic nature of the concept and specifically referring to productivity (and the oft suggested false dichotomy between productivity and the quality of work) maintains: "there is proof that progress in rights, in safety, working conditions and social dialogue frequently has a positive effect on employment and productivity, providing that institutional conditions are favourable".[16]

One of the challenges in this context is developing training instruments for employed ("active") personnel in line with technological and market requirements, thus contributing to improved productivity and working conditions, especially for vulnerable groups in these new circumstances. Sugar mill workers with the characteristics described above, living in rural areas with few alternative employment options, were considered a vulnerable group.

Whenever employment was affected by the productivity strategy adopted, or just by market adjustments, we could fall back on the occupational retraining programmes offered by the Labour Secretariat, that consisted of training scholarships or grants for laid off workers. In this way we had planned – at least in theory – a strategy to counter a possible "technological unemployment".

With this sugar industry background, a pilot experience with the ProMES model was decided on for a refinery, within the framework of the technical cooperation between the ILO and the STyPS, through the latter's CIMO programme. This was done at the request of the human resources' director of the corporation to which the refinery belonged, that had solicited support to design and apply a programme for the effective training of its personnel.

The main concern was to change the work culture, so that workers, middle managers and management might join efforts in one direction, i.e. the ongoing improvement of production processes and working conditions.

The existing work culture was characterised by a great diversity of perceptions and actions, few shared meanings, uncertainty of the personnel and a practice of reacting to events. In daily life this was reflected in a low level of commitment by workers to the company's objectives. They expected to be told what to do and to be supervised; they seldom undertook tasks outside their job description. They lacked a sense of the hygiene and cleanliness required by a food industry, or of the care they should take of themselves, the facilities and tools.

16 Rodgers, Gerry: *"Training, productivity and decent work"* (*Decent work as a goal for the global economy*). Montevideo, Cinterfor/ILO, n.153, 2002.

The project of promoting a new work culture in sugar mills was based on the assumption that efforts and resources devoted to technical/vocational training are of little avail unless the work culture is changed. The key question was: how to change the work culture? Before starting with ProMES the enterprise had offered some courses on human relations at work, and positive attitudes regarding communication and teamwork. They had not had the expected impact, largely because what was taught in the classroom had not been followed up later. As opposed to technical competencies, social abilities require unlearning previous habits and beliefs, which needs systematic follow-up.

Changing the work culture means trying to change values embedded in a consistent and integrated network of beliefs and understandings that tend to maintain the *status quo* (Schoenberger, 1997). Consequently, it is not a rapid or straightforward process, as it meets several types of resistance. Managing a change in the work culture breaking away from customary pathways, implies identifying and surmounting areas of resistance. This was an important task in managing the all-inclusive learning model. The difficulty is achieving a lasting change of attitude when conviction by knowledge or direct enforcement (by sanction or punishment) is not enough. "If there is no true persuasion or change of attitudes

---

PROJECT FOR A NEW WORK CULTURE IN SUGAR MILLS

- Active personnel involvement; promotion of shared meanings;

- Ongoing personnel training by occupational competencies;

- Creating favourable environment for learning and generating contextualised knowledge; socialising it in the organisation;

- Broadening and enriching workers' functions;

- Inclination towards flexibility and self-management of learning;

- Support of hygiene, safety and food health policies;

- Ongoing improvement, with mutual commitments between workers and the enterprise;

- High performance, self-managed teamwork.

---

and values, lasting, long-term behaviour can hardly be achieved. (....) the forms of influencing attitudes and values have to do with participation schemes. The problem is that such schemes are slower to implant, although they may ensure better long-term results" (Ronco; Lladé, 2000).

The image of the new work culture we sought was not quite clear. What *was* clear was that the existing culture had become an obstacle, a hitch for turning the sugar mill into a learning organisation capable of facing the challenges of current conditions. Revamping the situation for successfully meeting market demands and the workers' needs for development and welfare, would be the general picture of the new culture we visualised.

Its components were developed according to changing strategies and realities. Insofar as possible, our objective was to promote the active involvement of the everyday operations personnel, with the commitment of implementing improvements and the backing of the enterprise. The first and perhaps most important step towards change, was getting workers listened to by management and the other way round, getting them to listen to the suggestions of directors and middle mangers. From there we were able to build mutual commitments to support learning in the direction of constant improvement. That was the proposal of the ProMES model.

Application pathways

Application began in 1996 at the "Bellavista" sugar mill that in the crop season employs some three hundred people, that go down to two hundred in the period of repairs. The plant dates back from the early nineteen hundreds and has undergone technological changes through decisions devoid of medium or long-term planning. They have responded to partial needs, by area or sub-area, without any master plan.

In the years preceding the ProMES experiment, investments of approximately U$S 6 million had been made in the mill, mainly to increase processing capacity. They had had problems with the learning curve of the new equipment, mainly due to bad communications between management and the operatives. In view of increasing overproduction and a decline in market prices of sugar there was a threat of having to close down the mill unless it managed to improve operational costs in the short term. The abatement of idle periods (that accounted for nearly 20% of sugar-making time) was one of the immediate objectives for brining down costs. ProMES was supposed to contribute to that objective.

Another goal of ProMES was to reduce the accident rate. In 1995, thirty seven persons had been injured. The use of personal safety implements (helmets, shoes, goggles) was practically nil.

A factor influencing accidentality was the high degree of absenteeism caused by personnel turnover among different areas and the engagement of inexperienced workers.

As this was the first time for the enterprise and for the external CIMO and ILO consultants, we opted for a controlled application strategy, beginning by one shift in the mills area. The model was tried out during the 5 or 6 months of crop time and the evaluation was positive. Initially, the presence of the external consultants at the mill was constant, which enabled us to fine-tune the model and adapt it to the needs of the enterprise.

The following season the model was extended to all three shifts in the mills area, and in subsequent years to all areas, including field work. In general there was no reluctance of workers to take part, despite the fact that feedback meetings were held outside working hours. The only department that objected was mechanical maintenance. Mechanics knew that operation of the mill depended on them to a large extent. There was a struggle for power and leadership between mechanics –forged in practice and knowledgeable about equipment– and technicians in executive positions. To this were added internal differences that hindered adoption of the ProMES model. Maintenance was the last department to accept it.

ProMES PROGRESS	
Quantitative progress	Universe:
1995: 1 Shift 1 Area Bellavista Mill	(approx.: 35 persons)
1999: All Areas Bellavista Mill	(approx.: 245 persons)
2001: All Areas 4 Mills	(approx.: 1500 persons)
2002: All Areas 5 Mills; Beginning 1 Mill	(approx.: 1900 persons)
Accelerated learning introduction:	Beginning: 4 years to reach all areas
	Current: ½ to 1 year to reach all areas

PERSON / HOUR TRAINING COST ProMES vs. TRADITIONAL MODEL

Cost

Traditional training

ProMes

Person / hours training

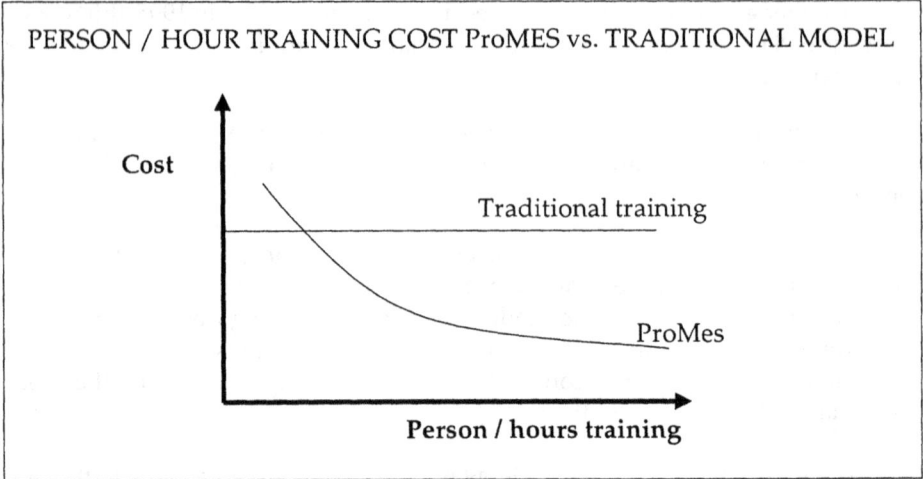

Insofar as the model met managerial and corporate expectations, resources for its support were allocated: a classroom, a computer and overhead projector, social amenities and prizes at the end of the cycle; meals at feedback boards and, above all, payment for the coordinator's time. By 2002 it was reckoned that direct application costs of the model (including prizes but not the time devoted by the coordinator and managers to the process) during the crop season were around U$S 15 thousand (less than 0.01% of gross sales). Taking an average of eight feedback board meetings with 80% attendance, the cost per person/hour would be about 4 dollars, which means an investment of 64 dollars per person during the 5 to 6 months of the season.

Costs are higher during start-up owing to investments in equipment and facilities and external counselling. As organisations take over the methodology, person/hour costs diminish. As opposed to traditional training in which person/hour costs remain constant when the number of participants increases, in ProMES costs go down when more persons join in. This is due to the scale economy effect of process standardisation. While traditional training is envisaged as a "product" (service) expressed in cost per person and per hour, ProMES training is a process with an initial cost that goes down in time and as more people are included. This makes it a viable proposal for ongoing training and learning at enterprises, from a costs point of view.

It is also viable from the point of view of results. Evaluation after the first year of application at the "Bellavista" mill showed positive results of a tangible and intangible kind. Among the tangible ones was a reduction of idle time attributable to operational errors by workers, fewer accidents and improved sanitary facilities. The intangibles were more and better communications between middle managers and workers, greater personnel co-operation and more proposals for improvement, enhanced labour atmosphere and ideas and explanations shared between operatives and middle managers.

Results became consolidated as the model was applied in different areas and departments of the plant which, together with its low costs, induced the human resources' management of the corporation to extend the "Bellavista" experience to the other three sugar mills it owned.

The underlying theories to be proved in this stage of institutional learning were basically two. The first one was that the ProMES model was suitable for, and could be adapted to the various occupational contexts of the sugar industry. The second one was that the learning accumulated in the first experience (whose tangible parts were formats – documentation and data processing – and procedures – schedule of feedback meetings, invitations, closing meetings, awards criteria) could be transferred to the other sugar mills to speed up the learning process (accelerated learning).

Both assumptions were confirmed. In spite of differences in occupational culture among the four refineries ("Bellavista" and the other three mills), the model could be adapted to the particular situation of each one. This shows that it is a valid proposal for this industry, characterised by a large number of structural obstacles to a continuous training strategy.

ProMES PROGRESS

Qualitative progress
- Procedures and formats:
  - Plant, field, admin.
  - Registration formats
  - Data processing
  - Awards criteria
  - Symbols: triptych, T-shirt, get-together
- Definition of coordination functions
- Constant update of indicators according to strategic objectives:
  - Volume; Costs; Quality; Haccp; ISO
  - Working conditions

Learning: Developing a robust model

The second hypothesis tried to establish how far application of the model could be accelerated, on the basis of the technical inputs from the first experience. In the first case it took four years to reach all areas; we managed to shorten that period to one year and a half. Attempts to shorten it further failed. Technical know-how ("typical application pathway") derived from a successful experience ("Bellavista") helped to bring down application time to one third. However, that seems to be the limit, for in each new instance the model needs to be adapted to the particular organisational culture to have effects upon it. It is a unique and complex process transforming inter-personal relations, and cannot therefore be implemented mechanically. It is time consuming due not only to cognitive difficulties but to social and cultural problems.

We verified that it was possible to accelerate application. Nevertheless, it was not quite clear whether this covered the whole pathway or just part of it, enough to proceed without petering out. This happened because firm anchoring of the model in the organisational culture could hardly be speeded up. The technical side of the process was liable to apparent acceleration, in the sense that the pathway was laid out. But that did not guarantee or speed up organisational or individual learning processes.

At the same time, it was shown that the model adapted easily to the new demands of the surrounding environment (marketplace, technologies, policies) that emerged in the six years of ProMES application. Increased processing capac-

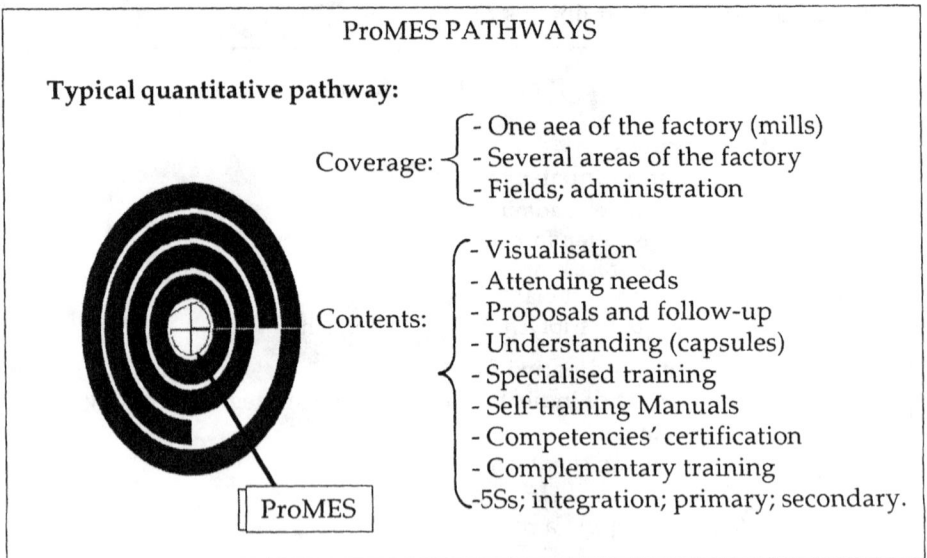

ProMES PATHWAYS

Typical quantitative pathway:

Coverage:
- One aea of the factory (mills)
- Several areas of the factory
- Fields; administration

Contents:
- Visualisation
- Attending needs
- Proposals and follow-up
- Understanding (capsules)
- Specialised training
- Self-training Manuals
- Competencies' certification
- Complementary training
- 5Ss; integration; primary; secondary.

ProMES

ity, that had for years been the industry's central concern ceased to be the main criterion for the success of sugar mills. Cost and quality were added, and especially compliance with Good Manufacturing Practices, one of the components of the international HACCP standard of food safety. ProMES proved very useful for implementation of the ISO 9000 and HACCP quality systems. Such systems require the ongoing participation and training of operational personnel, that under ProMES is carried out "naturally".

Further proof of adaptability was furnished by coordination of the model with other training programmes, like the 5Ss (technique of Japanese origin for keeping workplaces orderly and clean by means of five processes, all of them beginning with the letter "S"), specialised training and evaluation by competencies. In this broader spectrum ProMES remains the anchor programme, ensuring that other initiatives keep constantly in line with its objectives.

This has shown that the ProMES model not only retains its validity in different contexts, but also along time. It proved its soundness and relevance by acclimatising to changes in the environment that resulted in new strategic objectives for organisations. It showed its firmness in surviving political / institutional changes. In 2001, when the four sugar mills where ProMES was being applied were expropriated and became State property, the process was not discontinued.

In the subsequent expansion stage (2001-2002), the hypotheses to be proved referred to the model's sustainability and effectiveness. The TVET institutions involved (as well as the Labour Secretariat, STyPS) had withdrawn their support a couple of years earlier. As from 2001 the Conocer and also the ILO considered that the project should be self-sustaining. By mid-2002 everything indicated that the mills themselves were defraying the costs implied by operation of the model, including the contracting of external consultants to follow up and extend training proposals.

The second hypothesis referred not only to expanding the accelerated learning generated in the three sugar mills in the previous stage, but also whether organisations valued the results of it. In other words, showing that there was a positive and effective cost/benefit relation. This could be demonstrated directly through measurements and calculations, or indirectly, by considering external counselling on a commercial basis.

The latter was in effect done as from 2002, when the TVET institutions and the ILO discontinued their subsidies. The ILO did not altogether pull out of the project, but considered that its role should now be the promotion of meta-learning, i.e. knowledge of how institutions and organisations learn.

RESULTS OF THE ProMES/OCCUPATIONAL COMPETENCIES MODEL
IN "ALIANZA POPULAR"

1. Greater communication and mutual trust between Workers and Supervisors
2. Cleaner and safer working areas
3. Improved labour relations
4. Greater awareness and participation by workers in the use of social protection equipment
5. Greater awareness of workers about the hygiene of products
6. Greater participation by workers in achieving area objectives
7. Greater responsibility of supervisors in accident prevention
8. Greater attention by upper managers to solving workers' problems
9. Increased personnel training (equipment operation, maintenance and safety)

The new sugar mills joining that year in application of the ProMES model showed not only that acceleration techniques were valid, but could be implemented with fewer resources than in the first multiplier experience. In that first case, constant external counselling was required for half a year (some 900 hours) to promote and document processes. In the second, multiplier phase external counselling went down to 80 hours in the first six months. That seems to be the threshold of external advice that organisations like sugar refineries need in the start-up stage.

Four key stages were identified in the application of ProMES, each one with its respective critical aspects (see synoptic Table). They are necessary though not sufficient requirements for the successful completion of each stage.

It is difficult to keep the model optimally in line with the organisation's policies, and to obtain active personnel participation all the time and throughout all phases of implementation. Experience has shown that application has ups and downs. It is quite "natural" that after start-up and through initial momentum, a peak in participation should be reached as well as coincidence with the organisation's strategy. However, when the novelty has worn out, it is not unusual to see a decline. There is a risk of falling into an unproductive routine at feedback meetings.

ProMES PATHWAYS

Typical qualitative pathway:

Key stages	**Critical aspects**
• Start-up	*Securing the support of actors and defining Coordination*
• Consolidation	*Coaching Coordination, defining formats, routines*
• Development	*Improving formats, routines and group dynamics*
• Renewal	*Periodically adopting new indicators; deepening training; extending to other tools*

The upkeep of the ProMES model depends on a capacity for going deeper into things, extending them and renewing them. The model must avoid becoming an instrument of the *status quo*, a valueless routine.

There is a moment when it comes up against the *counterculture* that intends to reclaim lost ground. The model may then be caught up in the mesh of the culture of the past and its related interests, in the midst of a constant struggle for the organisation's identity. There are permanent questionings about why change what is being done "if it was always done like that". Doubts and criticisms crop up, some more justified than others. In the case of sugar mills such criticism did not necessarily embody a different view of modernity but just a wish to return to past practices. The result of this struggle and cultural contraposition is not always favourable for ProMES schemes, but is decisive in establishing the course of change to be followed by the organisational culture.

It may also happen that the department or the whole plant goes into a crisis that has nothing to do with the model. If the phenomenon is not remedied in time, the model can be threatened by imminent collapse.

It has been estimated that the longer and deeper the fall, the greater the effort needed to recover the group dynamics of the scheme. When telltale symptoms become apparent in a model, as a result of exhaustion, counterculture or external crisis, it will be necessary to reinforce interventions by the coordinator and external counsellors. Action beyond direct application of the ProMES model

ProMES PATHWAYS

peak

Integration of
model into
organisational
strategy

Degree of
personnel
participation

decline

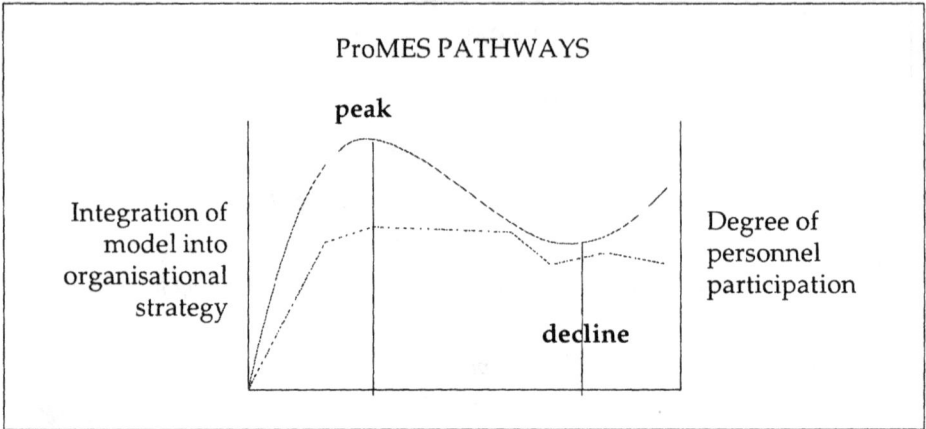

is sometimes required to re-establish normal operational conditions. For instance, re-structuring working areas, reappointing persons or reallocating functions, or simply waiting for the market to resume its normal course.

Not all problems can be foreseen because some are unconnected with the model. Others, however, are intrinsic in the ProMES application pathway and good management can forestall them. For example, the wearing out of feedback boards because they do not tackle subjects in sufficient depth, or fail to establish a link between the workers' tacit knowledge and the coded knowledge of technicians or managers; non-adherence to commitments and reverting to the old work culture; management's conviction that problems must not be analysed with the workers, or inversely, the workers' persuasion that taking part in ProMES is equivalent to "selling out" to the bosses.

ProMES PROBLEMS / LIMITATIONS

Superficial learning

- Not going deep enough into subjects
- Running out of subjects
- Failing to blend coded and uncoded knowledge
- Becoming repetitive (not making progress...)
- Losing significance
- Failing to develop specialisations
- Reverting to the "old" work culture

In the Mexican experiment, institutional learning in connection with ProMES centred on a group of consultants depending on the ILO, the sugar mills involved and initially the CIMO programme. This programme never incorporated the ProMES methodology into its counselling offer, for it confined itself to the role of intermediary between small and medium enterprises with training needs and local consultants. It was not supposed to generate and apply training methodologies (Mertens, 2001). In addition, no programme has yet been developed for training trainers in the ProMES method, apart from the scheme's coordinators and the human resources' managers of the respective sugar mills.

b. Self-training and assessment guides by competencies in Mexico

Design of a training model by competencies using a self-study and assessment guide began at the "Bellavista" sugar mill in 1998, as a complement of the ProMES model. It had the institutional support of Conocer, CIMO, and the ILO, that shared counselling costs with the mill. The experience was one of the cases backed by Conocer to show that the occupational competencies' model was functional for managing human resources in organisations, in order to face new market demands and rapid technological and organisational changes.

Later on enterprises from other branches (electronics, commerce, garment industry) engaged in similar experiences. Nonetheless, the greatest progress in recent years has been made in a leading food company in Mexico and other Latin American countries. The experiences of the sugar mills, the food company and the garment industry are analysed below.

Sugar mills

The self-training/assessment guides were initially designed at the "Bellavista" mill. The low schooling of workers, their lack of reading habits and the proven ineffectiveness of schoolroom training, called for an accessible and significant instrument for delivering job-related knowledge to them.

We first developed a profile of key competencies and a description of performances and knowledge required. To that end we applied the SCID format to a group of supervisors and managers. Workers were not involved in this process. In the absence of operational manuals and to avoid further confusion, we opted for starting by standardising operational criteria among middle and upper managers.

Owing to the non-existence of manuals, the initial versions of competency standards were used as such, describing operations step by step. This was subsequently corrected by using broader descriptors of performances and knowledge.

Competencies' profiles and standards were very useful for drafting the manual. They enabled us to maintain consistency through the process and acted as checklists for sequence and control purposes.

Our initial strategy was to develop a modular manual based on the key competencies of the mills area. As we proceeded through the seven modules (for as many key competencies) it became evident that only one of them should be specific to each area, namely, operating and watching over the production equipment. The contents of the other modules were applicable to all areas: maintaining equipment, lubricating parts, reading measurement parameters, working under safety standards, working by objectives, contributing to teamwork.

Each guide includes self-assessment, a technical explanation and an instrument for assessing knowledge and performance. Besides being a training tool, it is an assessment instrument. This turns it into a record for certification purposes. Everything is thus bundled together in a single instrument, which makes it easier for the enterprise and the workers.

After finishing the guides, we proceeded to draft a procedures manual of the process of training and assessing by competencies. That was the main requirement for the enterprise to be accredited as assessment centre by the national certifying body authorised to certify personnel according to the national technical standard for sugar making.

As the enterprise standard did not have the same architecture as the national standard we had to draw up a table of performance and knowledge equivalencies. We pointed out that the enterprise standard covered and sometimes exceeded the requirements of the national standard. The certifying body accepted our argument. This showed that national technical standards could be interpreted with flexibility without detracting from their basic contents.

Having been granted accreditation as assessment centre, we started the evaluation and certification process by area supervisors and superintendents. The aim was to familiarise them with both experiences: evaluating and being evaluated, and training them in the methodology. Fifteen supervisors and superintendents were certified in the first stage. The second stage was applying the method to the workers. That process was interrupted when, for financial reasons, a group of twenty-nine sugar mills, the "Bellavista" among them, were taken over by the government. Interest in the evaluation and certification experiment waned, as the management was no longer under the pressure of the former corporate owners.

The "Bellavista" experience was transferred to another sugar mill, the "Alianza Popular", that was also accredited as evaluation centre. On this occasion the guides were adapted to an *ad hoc* format for use at ProMES feedback boards and give them wider scope. The "San Gabriel" plant used the guides in a similar way, although this third sugar mill was not accredited as evaluation centre.

For a number of reasons –among them lack of leadership and support by upper managers, and lack of incentives for workers to get certified, as their jobs are assured all the same– use of the guides has met with difficulties, as well as the consequent certification procedures. However, this does not mean that the project has been abandoned. Market demands for compliance with ISO quality models and HACCP food safety standards require proof of personnel competencies. This opens up a possibility for application of the guides and certification of workers in the short term.

Clothes making enterprises

Our experience in the garment industry started with the link of a TVET centre with an enterprise. Their objective was to train and evaluate workers in "quality management in the assembly of garments". This was a specific need the enterprise had to compete in the export market.

The proposal emphasised developing a guide rapidly, so we drafted it in a month's time. We used the SCID model of systematic curriculum development to collect all the information required for a self-contained guide. On the basis of digital technology (digital photographs) we managed in a short period (six working days – four weeks in practice due to interruptions for other activities -) to devise a guide focusing on a critical aspect for the enterprise, i.e. quality management.

In two sessions of 4 hours each we applied the SCID format to two of the company's garment assembly supervisors. It is important to describe the steps followed through this stage to understand the process for application in other contexts.

The first step was a tour of the facilities to get an idea of the different areas, flow of productive process and the products themselves.

A second step was a brief analysis of the strengths and weaknesses of the organisation. The enterprise director, the person in charge of quality and two supervisors of the garment assembly area were present in this exercise. Quality management in the productive process was pinpointed as the main weakness –as well as an opportunity area– in the productive process.

The third step was identification of the critical points of quality management of the process directly influenced by the operational manpower. The seven critical points, or processes identified were in connection with client satisfaction and these seven sub-competencies make up the key competency of the enterprise, called *quality management in the assembly of garments.*

The fourth step was application of the SCID format to the two supervisors, which consisted of systematically compiling information on the expected performance standard, the equipment utilised for reaching that standard, the related knowledge, the safety aspects to be observed, the decisions workers had to make to attain the standard, typical errors to be avoided, the communication and attitudes required. In the case of attitudes, sometimes they are difficult to establish. Nevertheless, it is clearer to determine what must not be evinced, or is to be avoided. This fourth step is fundamental in the experience, because training and assessment actions are derived from it.

The format was designed with a view to focusing on critical points, going deeper into them and with a concept of work going beyond the performance of a prescribed task and including unforeseen events, decisions, mistakes and attitudes. For that reason it is important to ensure that respondents (in this instance the two women supervisors) are qualified and concentrated on the items in the format. The involvement of an external expert at this stage proved to be very useful for interpreting the process.

The fifth step consisted of taking digital photos of the production process, of each one of the aspects indicated in the SCID format for the preceding step. Here it is important that the qualified respondents –the two supervisors in this case– point out the details of what is to be photographed to serve as reference in the training. Once information had been compiled according to the SCID format, we began preparation of the self-training guide. We should underline that the success of the compiling stage depends to a great extent on the *rate and flexibility* of the process. It is essential that the qualified respondents should not get overtired, since that affects the quality of the information obtained.

The self-training guide consists of three parts. Each one of the guide's sections –self-diagnosis, explanation and assessment– is based on the information gathered in the SCID format. Their structure is similar to that of the format, which facilitates matters. Close correlation must be kept between the three parts. In the explanation section trainees will find the necessary information to complete their self-diagnosis. In the assessment part, they will clearly see the form and contents of the assessments, in line with the self-diagnosis and explanation.

This stage is laborious and it consumed most of the time devoted to the experience. It requires human resources and a sufficiently powerful computerised equipment to process the information based on digital photos. We recommend preparing guides that can be easily adapted for direct use and electronic visual presentation.

After completing the first version of the guide, we proceeded to validate it, which is essential for ensuring quality and relevance. Validation is implemented in two moments. Initial validation is done by a group of "experts", in this case the two supervisors. The second validation is by a group of workers that try the guide out.

The guide was reviewed and corrected in 4 hours' time by the same two supervisors and a technician from the training institute. A portable computer and a projector provided vital technological support for this task *(data show)*.

Corrections were made while the guide was being projected on a screen, and the first version was finalised. The technology stepped up the procedure and once again prevented the boredom of tiredness of the group of "experts".

The subsequent stage was application of the guides by pilot groups of five women workers in each department. The two supervisors acted as instructors and evaluators. To make the process more fluent we decided that the workers would cover only the more general part of client satisfaction and the cluster of operations involved. We did not implement certification by national standards.

In this instance we showed that the whole process of producing a training-assessment guide could be abbreviated to two or three weeks. That gave rise to the concept of *"express guides"* that was later used in garment enterprises of the Dominican Republic and northern Mexico.

The guide was used in the garment industry in northern Mexico because they needed a training instrument for managing quality at the source, i.e. during actual production.

The market context was one of uncertainty. Market conditions had become increasingly stringent: price reduction (between 20 and 30%), and greater demands for quality. As compared to the year before, employment had shrunk by more than 50% (at the moment of drafting the guide, about one thousand persons were working in two factories). The guide was going to be used both by employed workers and newly engaged recruits. The scheme had the support of the STyPS / ILO Project "More and better jobs for women".

Start-up comprised two key stages. The first one was explaining the goals, characteristics and scope of the proposal to the management, and securing their approval and participation. The second one was to incorporate the proposal into the functions of a group of persons in the enterprise, with clear-cut responsibilities and the backing of upper management.

In connection with the first stage, we invited managers and directors of the company (fifteen persons) to an introductory meeting. We submitted to them the proposal for a training and evaluation manual on quality management and working conditions, based on previous experiences. It coincided with the enterprise's need to raise its quality levels (its final percentage of rejects in internal quality inspections was of 2.5 to 4%) and bring down manufacturing costs, by reassigning tasks of responsibility to men and women operatives. We agreed to work jointly (enterprise and project) in drafting a training and evaluation manual on quality management and enhancement of working conditions. This was in line with the code of ethics of the company and the social and legal standards that the client (in this case a prestigious make of clothing) required of its suppliers.

COMPETENCIES

General

- Client satisfaction
- Working under safety standards
- Contributing to the care and preservation of equipment
- Maintaining order and cleanliness
- Effective communication
- An attitude of collaboration and teamwork
- Caring for your hygiene and health
- Helping to promote equal opportunities for men and women

Specific

- Joining upper piece correctly
- Attaching hip pocket correctly
- Attaching rear pieces correctly
- Attaching inner leg pieces correctly
- Preparing waistband correctly
- Backstitching front pocket

Regarding the second start-up stage, we identified aspects that were critical for quality. Two meetings of 4 hours each were held with persons involved in quality management at different levels: quality manager, operations manager, process engineering, maintenance, supervisors and men and women workers. With this technical group we began by establishing in which operations the company had greater problems to meet the quality standards required by the client. Our universe was the trousers' assembly department. Six clusters of operations were identified as critical.

We applied the SCID format to each one of those operations. Analysing the first cluster we found several competencies of a generic type (communication, attitudes, cleanliness and order), which made the exercise more time consuming. Besides, general competencies were given wider scope, including equality of women and men. More rapid progress was made in subsequent sessions, for we focused only on specific competencies.

On the basis of the information gathered in the SCID format (most of it tacit knowledge of expert personnel, converted at feedback boards into coded knowledge, more easily grasped by the organisation) we proceeded to take digital photographs in the area and work stations. The photos and the information were the main inputs of the training and evaluation guides.

A fundamental aspect at this stage is establishing within the enterprise who will be in charge of coordinating the preparation and application of the manual. The responsibility was assigned to the human resources' area, due to its leadership in training initiatives. The manager of human resources (HR) was appointed general coordinator, while the training manager was made responsible for the drafting. They were both given the necessary equipment for the job (last generation computers).

Paradoxically, in the two enterprises of the garment industry the speed with which the guides were developed was not matched by their application. Management took a long time to decide implementing the process. In the second plant application was delayed by a change of management. Consequently, it is not enough for external experts to collaborate in preparing the instruments. They must also follow up their application, which consumes more energy and time than the actual preparation. In addition, resources are required and in this case they had not been provided for, so the enterprises had to partially and irresolutely continue under their own steam.

Food company

The company introduced management by occupational competencies in the logistics area through a project co-financed by Conocer. The purpose of Conocer in this undertaking was to produce demonstrative cases that might serve as an example for other enterprises. When the project came to an end late in 2001, we had succeeded in getting the enterprise to incorporate management by competencies into its organisational and personnel strategies. As from 2002, it is financing one hundred per cent of competencies' projects in several areas.

As opposed to the case of the garment industry, the design pathway of the model was long. The company had a high degree of systematisation and documentation of processes, which had yielded good results. Changing the system or introducing a new one required a sound proposal. However, that was not enough. Even a sound proposal was likely to meet with resistance among lovers of the existing scheme. We took the long pathway (three years) not only for technical reasons and/or the depth we wanted for the instrument, but to win over sufficient support and involvement from the various managers and directors whose areas would be affected by the proposal.

As the competencies' concept and methodology settled down in the organisation, the time it took to prepare instruments – profile, self-training and knowledge evaluation guide, performance formats and product evidence – was reduced considerably (by six months to one year).

The process started in the heavy transportation area. The objective was to devise a continuous learning instrument for operators to keep updated in their competency. They all had previous training as drivers of heavy-duty vehicles but through the years they lost precision in certain habits and key routines, like for instance regular checkups before, during and after trips. The instrument was intended to provide ongoing training for drivers in critical aspects for the efficient and safe handling of their vehicles. The expected results were lower operational costs and accident rates. In the medium term the process would help operators to get certification and qualify for international drivers' licenses.

A technical group of expert transport operators, supervisors and mechanics developed in the first place an enterprise competency standards with the Conocer format. These standards were subsequently corrected and validated by representatives of other companies and by the communications authorities, before becoming national technical competency standards issued by the Conocer.

The same technical group collaborated in establishing a baseline for the guide. A format was applied with critical routine aspects: unforeseen events, information inquiries and decision-making, specific safety, communication and attitudinal elements. After ten days of reflection and analysis we had enough information and practical material for preparing a draft version of the manual. Apart from generating inputs, those ten days constituted a training event for the personnel taking part. They also provided learning for the organisation, as several proposals for improving processes came out of them.

The manual modules cover the competencies' profile or standards. Two modules are technical (transport review and efficient & safe driving), another one refers to administrative management and communication (links with other areas), and the last one is social and personal (integral health). They reflect an overall view of competencies in which performance is the result of a number of organisational and personal factors.

The draft was revised by the enterprise's specialised technical staff. This took too long, and the time assigned by the specialist to work with the manual was limited. Besides, specialists changed several times. All this showed that the organisation did not yet have a clear idea of the scope and meaning of the project.

An interesting thing at this stage was that as in the other cases described earlier, upper and middle managers did not entirely agree about operational procedures and criteria. Opinions differed about the performance and knowledge required. At this point, a uniformity of criteria was reached among the directive staff involved with the project.

As a complement to the printed manual, an interactive compact disk (CD) was issued. The aim was to reinforce cognitive learning without adding more hours of classroom training. The disk also serves for evaluating knowledge more economically as trainees are asked to complete the CD, that is designed in such a way that no progress can be made without having digested the preceding topics. When candidates have finalised, this is automatically recorded in a database. The supervisor or instructor can then rapidly detect who has finished the task well, and who requires further help.

Making the CD also took its time, partly because the layout had to be designed. We had no experience in designing a CD by competencies. The two months initially set aside for the task ran into ten, for several reasons, which included technical programming hitches, problems in the enterprise computer system and changes in the design of the CD itself.

We were not quite sure about the reactions to the CD of very senior workers, with low levels of schooling and little or no experience in the use of computers. In the pilot runs we saw that those people required initial assistance, but then became quite enthusiastic.

The next instrument was performance evaluation by observation and concrete results (fuel consumption, accident rate, care of the vehicle, etc.) Competency levels were introduced here: entrance level (driving in the company yard), driving in town and on the highway.

The sum total of the three instruments (the manual, the CD and performance assessment) are the basis for constant learning in this area of the organisation. For the learning to be an effectively ongoing and continuous process, we introduced a dynamics of yearly cycles. The cycle starts with an initial assessment. On the basis of its results, drivers and evaluators (supervisors) jointly work out a training plan. Workers have to provide evidence on agreed items before the final assessment of the cycle. If their score is sufficient, they qualify for the respective certification. Nevertheless, in the following cycle they resume the assessment and learning process and have to produce fresh evidence to qualify for further certification.

This scheme intends to keep up the learning dynamics within the organisation, together with other mechanisms like the specialisation courses offered by suppliers of equipment and engines. Certification is done through an internal verification in the working area and an "internal-external" checkout by the corporate owners.

We did not opt for external certification by a certifying body accredited with the Conocer, although internally we very closely followed Conocer assessment-certification guidelines. Perhaps a fear of the excessive red-tape and bureaucratic complications entailed by external certification, and extra costs with no visible added value advantages were the main reasons for opting for internal, company certification. Workers were not affected, because if they changed over to another organisation their certificates were backed by the company's prestige in the transport business. Nonetheless, it is quite likely that external certification may be adopted in the future in connection with standardised drivers' licenses and permits, particularly in connection with traffic into the USA.

After the design stage of instruments in accordance with the organisation's operation, culture and systems, there was a very important question mark: how did we incorporate the more than one thousand existing transport workers into the process? The only answer was by training facilitators and evaluators. For that purpose we developed a trainers' training programme by competencies. It consists of a guide of performance-related knowledge for facilitators-evaluators. The guide includes a training and assessment procedures manual, and the competencies' profile of internal evaluators and verifiers. Two groups of twenty-five trainers (that included area managers, supervisors and expert operatives) met during three days each to work with the guide and the transport workers' training and evaluation instruments (manual, CD and performance evaluation). Once participants had shown their capacity to train and evaluate transport workers, they prepared a personal evidence file and were qualified for the facilitator-evaluator certificates issued by the company.

With this we expect to extend application of the model to all the organisation, keeping the quality of the process. The proposal for training, evaluating and certifying trainers is in line with directives followed by the Conocer. The only difference with the Conocer trainers' training model is adaptation to the situation, needs and language of the organisation.

As a result of this experience the company decided to extend training by competencies to other areas, like sales and manufacturing, but it did not opt for the same detailed methodology. Although the method has a great deal in common with functional analysis and Dacum/SCID, the different areas were given leeway to adapt it to their respective needs and culture (Mertens, 2000). What was established as a common model for all the enterprises were the stages of the process: profile; training manual and assessment of related knowledge; performance assessment instruments; guide of training, assessment, verification and certification procedures; training and assessment of facilitators, evaluators and verifiers; application, evaluation and improvement of the model.

Progress and application problems of self-training and assessment guides

In the 1997-2002 five-year period, quantitative progress has been recorded in the application of the self-training and evaluation guides' methodology. Although in no case did application extend to all the population envisaged by the proposal, by mid-2002 the projected universe of operational personnel and supervisors involved in the process was over twenty-five thousand persons.

Learning was accomplished in the design of profiles and training and assessment manuals, shortening the time required from three years to one or even half a year. However, learning still to be achieved is accelerated application in the projected universe. Qualitative progress paves the ground for quantitative development. The model's proposal was bolstered by the progress of its basic components.

SELF-TRAINING / ASSESSMENT PROGRESS

Quantitative progress	Projected universe:
2000: Sugar Mill (1)	(approx. 200 persons)
2001: Sugar Mills (3)	(approx. 745 persons)
2001: Garment industry (1)	(approx. 65 persons)
2002: Garment industry (2)	(approx. 1000 persons)
2002: Food industry (3)	(approx. 2500 persons)

Accelerated Learning Introduction:	**Beginning:** 3 years to design profiles, manuals
	Currently: ½ to 1 year for profile, manual.

The model's conceptual and methodological framework has been adapted to the needs of organisations. Its views and strategies can easily adjust to their specific requirements.

Self-training / assessment has proved to be a flexible process under either formal or informal conditions, which organisations have accepted with interest. The proposal is in line with the latest versions of ISO quality standards and is a

---

SELF-TRAINING / ASSESSMENT PROGRESS

Qualitative progress:
- Conceptual and methodological development
- Procedures and formats:
  - Profile
  - Performance assessment instrument
  - Knowledge assessment instrument; CD
  - Procedures manual
  - Trainers' training manual

- Acceptance Self-assessment; links with ISO and FTAA
- Definition of process and functions
- Adaptation to specific needs of organisations

Learning: Developing robust model

---

forerunner of homologation of certain qualifications in the frame of the Free Trade Agreement of the Americas (FTAA) that will have strategic importance in the medium term for some sectors (*eg.* transportation and foodstuffs).

There are examples of the formats and basic procedures that have been tried out (profile, training and performance and knowledge assessment, process procedures, trainers' training). By defining the process and respective functions of the personnel involved, an adaptation can be offered to organisations according to their needs, without jeopardising consistency or unnecessarily lengthening the process. The model can be mass produced and tailored to each organisation.

Despite progress made, there is still a number of problems to solve for the proposal to be viable for organisations and an unobjectionable instrument for improving productivity and working conditions.

The main problems encountered (which are in turn areas of opportunity for institutional learning) are the following:

1.   The pathway to reach workers is long. As time goes by, enthusiasm wanes in the organisation and the proposal's priority may be eroded by other projects and emerging needs.

2.   A just balance has to be struck between perfection and pragmatism in the design of instruments and application process. There is a risk of excessive desk work in search of the perfection of each stage, instead of visualising the

---

SELF-TRAINING/ASSESSMENT PROBLEMS

- Lengthy pathway: cost, loss of enthusiasm
- Perfectionism vs. pragmatism
- Understanding the methodology; differences with traditional training
- Contradictions among workers about coding
- Attitudes of contempt towards tacit knowledge
- Resistance of middle managers to change in their functions; new responsibilities, transfer of other duties
- Reproduction costs
- Change of work and control systems
- Systemic interrelation with other HR areas: selection, remuneration, promotion
- Difficulty and resistance of operational personnel to the proposal

---

proposal as a process of constant adaptation and improvement. This also implies a danger, i.e. going into a process of constant and aimless change. It is therefore essential to have a mechanism for checking up modifications as they are introduced.

3. The methodology breaks away from traditional training schemes. Understanding the change of training paradigm is not a straightforward process in the mind of the organisation's directors and managers. There is always the risk of reverting to traditional ways when implementation difficulties crop up, or when problems appear in other areas like the marketplace, financing or labour relations. In such circumstances, vision of the project may be lost in favour of the easy solution, i.e. giving up on it.

4. Development of the profile and training manuals, structure and implicit curriculum is not based on the theoretical logics of process engineering but on practice, on productive realities. A large part of it consists of coding the good practices used by workers, which are not always evident. The opposite to this is equally important: what deviates from established policies and procedures. The risk here is in two directions. The first one is that the technical personnel may not duly appreciate the importance of good tacit practices, and should impose the logics of theory. The second one is that the wrong routines and practices should be coded. Therefore, the challenge is to understand the tension between these two extremes and strike the right balance between them.

5. The model implies new functions for middle and upper managers. They are usually reluctant to accept them, because they see them as an additional burden and not an opportunity to exert their leadership and meet the goals that have been ascribed to them. The danger is that they may be the first to discourage workers from co-operating with the model, belittling its importance and stressing that there are more immediate and pressing needs. This is also related to another cause for resistance, namely a change in the work system and in the exercise of power and control. The model will make evident capabilities (or the lack thereof) in the managing staff, which will arouse their resistance or support of it. The challenge is to identify this situation early on in the process, to facilitate introduction of the model and avoid wasting energy in a search for solutions that may not be relevant.

6. There is also resistance among workers, particularly when there are promotion and selection systems favouring job seniority over capabilities, or when employees are near retirement age and see no advantage in investing time or energy in application of the model. They may also fear the loss of a leader-

ship that is not based on capabilities but on interests. The risk is that such individuals may dissuade their companions or even handle the proposal politically, arguing that it is a disguised reallocation of functions that must be opposed. The challenge here is twofold: on the one hand, we have to re-value occupational qualification and let the personnel know it. On the other hand, we must not give in to the temptation of modifying the essential contents of functions without prior agreement with the parties involved.

7. The moment when the training by competencies model should be connected with other sub-systems in human resources management is a key decision for the sustainability of the introduction process. Pretending to link up all the sub-systems of HR management (especially compensations) with the competencies model from the very beginning, entails the possibility of getting lost in the intricacies of each sub-system, and slowing down introduction of the model by imminent danger of losing control of the process. All the same, we must keep in mind that in the middle term points of contact will have to be found between the various HR management sub-systems and competencies' management, in order to achieve the desired impact and convey consistent signs to the organisation and its personnel.

8. The cost of the process is a factor that must be handled in accordance with the organisation's possibilities and policies. The reproduction of training guides is an expense that not all organisations are prepared to accept, or in a position to defray. The process may come to a halt for that reason. There are many ways of handling costs. Backing by high management is essential, but so is flexibility of design to find more economic alternatives with a minimum loss of quality in the training process.

The problems and challenges outlined above continue to be pending, but they provide an idea of the competencies required for successfully managing and putting in place the proposed model.

Institutional learning in the cases that have been described was confined to those in charge and the internal and external consultants involved, some of them connected with the ILO. Originally, there was a functional link with Mexican TVET institutes, especially the Conocer, the CIMO programme and some state training bodies. Those organisations underwent significant changes when the new political administration took over in 2001. In order not to waste previous efforts, we decided to proceed with cases already under way and subsequently renew our connection with projects, programmes and organisations of the national technical/vocational education and training system (TVET).

From another point of view, the fact that cases originally supported by the Conocer and CIMO have continued, is an indication of the institutional learning that has been achieved. One of the objectives in assisting these enterprises was to generate significant demonstrative cases that might encourage others to follow the example. That was achieved, helping to strengthen the institutionality of occupational competencies as a system of signs and symbols among the social actors. That interpretation meant leaving aside the view that automatically associates institutional learning with established public bodies. What we are suggesting here is an institutional view nearer to the concept of culture, with the joint participation of pubic and private institutions and civil society through individual and collective leaderships. The risk of such an interpretation lies in the difficulty of fully gauging its scope and overseeing its evolution, which may turn it into a virtual rather than a real thing, based on hardly justifiable explanations if there are no clear, unobjectionable indicators.

c. ProMES in the Dominican Republic: an integral view of productivity

In 1997, the National Technical/Vocational Training Institute (Spanish acronym: Infotep) of the Dominican Republic started application of an integral instrument for measuring and improving productivity, one of whose four main components was ProMES. The other three components referred to the economic/financial, productive and individual performance of the organisation in question.

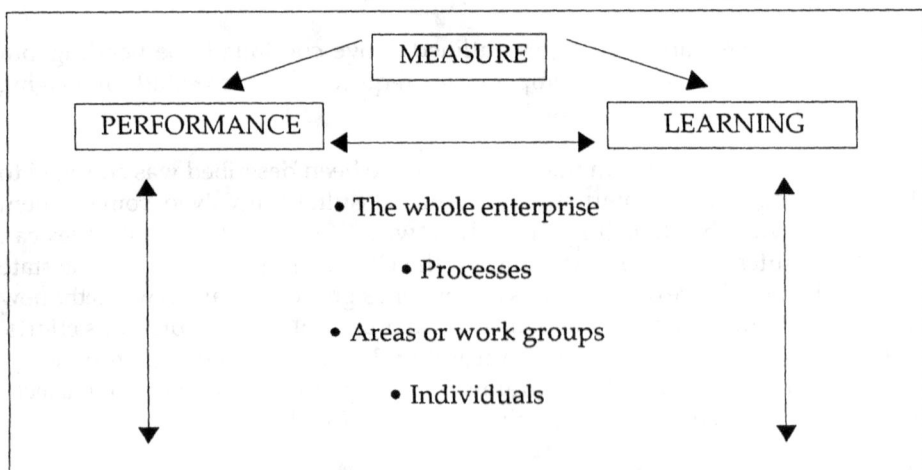

The integral view is based on the following assumption: unless performance is measured as an input / product relation on the various strategic planes of the organisation, efforts made to improve any one indicator may be lost or counter-productive.

The main problem is not measuring and generating indicators, but understanding the position of each indicator in relation to the final results expected in the pursuit of objectives.

Having established the four strategic levels or planes on which organisations learn, measurements on each one of them provide information that has to become new understanding, which is in turn the basis for productivity. The diagnosis that gave rise to this overall methodological proposal was that most small and medium-sized Dominican enterprises lacked enough consistent information on those four planes. In such circumstances, the proposal of the ProMES methodology of measuring the performance of working areas or groups would be limited unless supplemented by adequate measurement of other processes and of the enterprise as a whole.

However, it is not just a question of generating information. The challenge is turning it into understanding, and that understanding into fresh shared knowledge and productivity increments. The first step is measuring; the second one, turning the information obtained into an input for learning.

> *...knowledge is acquired through learning, and learning only occurs when there is understanding, and when new information leads to new understanding...*

The following is a brief description of the instrument's four components:

Integral Instrument for Productivity Measurement and Enhancement

a. Overall economic performance

By means of this instrument the organisation can draw up a permanent productivity diagnosis of its main processes and areas, and of its contribution to general productivity, which helps it to make decisions and follow up strategic plans. Indicators are expressed as an inputs / results ratio (both in monetary and physical terms) and go from the general to the specific along two lines: efficiency in the use of variable inputs (materials, manpower), and efficiency in the use of assets (machinery, equipment, facilities). They are represented on a map that shows their position with respect to each other and in the general picture. The instrument enables us to establish links among indicators and appreciate the economic evolution of the organisation.

An example of how establishing links between indicators helps in decision-making is the comparative intensiveness in the use of machinery and labour. An increase in manpower productivity through the introduction of new equipment does not necessarily raise the productivity of assets. It is important for the organisation to know how both indicators have behaved and how they have contributed to total productivity, defined as the return on assets (relation between operational benefits and operational assets).

This instrument will help us to visualise, control and guide the decision-making process, although it will not tell us exactly what to do. It will show us where the problems are and where progress has been made. It relates processes and physical decisions (production hours, number of persons engaged, amount of inputs used) to monetary variables (costs, benefits). It is a bridge between the sphere of work and that of finances.

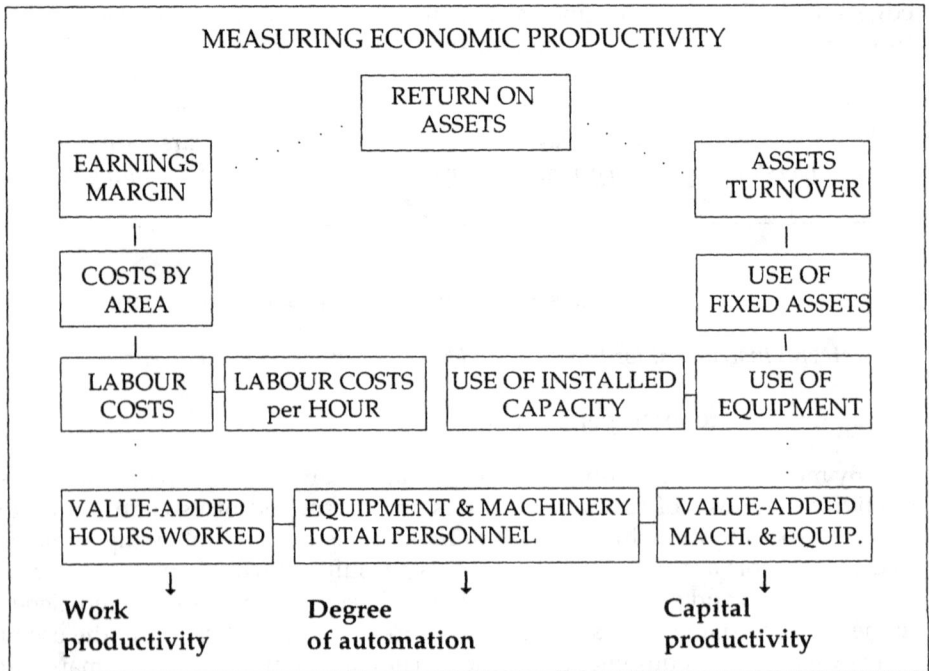

MEASURING ECONOMIC PRODUCTIVITY

RETURN ON ASSETS

EARNINGS MARGIN   ASSETS TURNOVER

COSTS BY AREA   USE OF FIXED ASSETS

LABOUR COSTS | LABOUR COSTS per HOUR | USE OF INSTALLED CAPACITY | USE OF EQUIPMENT

VALUE-ADDED HOURS WORKED | EQUIPMENT & MACHINERY TOTAL PERSONNEL | VALUE-ADDED MACH. & EQUIP.

Work productivity   **Degree of automation**   **Capital productivity**

It consists of about 30 indicators that each organisation can add to or reduce according to its needs, providing that the instrument's consistency is not impaired. The present instrument is an adaptation of the original model designed by Canadian consultant G. Rivest. That model was used in a Canadian programme that compared different enterprises in the same branch of activity to develop a benchmark for each indicator, as a way of encouraging organisational learning in the companies involved (Thor, 1993).

b. Performance of the productive process

The instrument for measuring the performance of the productive process is a number of indicators (21) expressing partial efficiencies in physical terms (hours, quantity, quality, response time). Its purpose is evaluating and promoting concrete learning in accordance with the organisation's strategic objectives. It is an instrument mainly utilised by upper and middle management to promote the strategic project of the organisation in relation to engineering, systems and human resources management.

These indicators are part of a broader self-diagnostic instrument used by directors, managers and middle managers. It traces out the organisation's competitiveness and productivity curves that enables directive staff to share results and standardise criteria regarding strategies and objectives.

The instrument is self-administered and answered by a nominal scale (yes; no) or a an ordinal scale (unimportant; scarcely important; important; very important). No exact figures are required, only approximations, which implies loss of accuracy but greater flexibility and less resistance of respondents to answer. It

---

MEASURING PRODUCTIVITY/PROCESS

Self-diagnostic instrument of Competitiveness
and Productivity pathways

Sections:

- Competitive profile
- Productivity indicators
- Productivity objectives and problems
- Innovation initiatives
- Problems in Human Resources Management

---

was designed in the framework of the project "Technological Change and the Labour Market" jointly sponsored by the ILO and the Canadian International Development Agency (CIDA) and tried out in more than five hundred enterprises in Latin America in the 90s´. It was devised on the basis of an international research project on best practices in the organisation and management of human resources in the manufacturing sector. However, many of its sections– specially the one about diagnosing problems in the management of human resources and working conditions– are not exclusively applicable to the manufacturing sector or to a given period in time. This makes the instrument valid in a diversity of contexts, particularly when it is used flexibly and in accordance with the realities of each organisation.

The evolution of employment quality is also dealt with in the section on problems in human resources management. It envisages about 16 categories with several elements each.

With this instrument´s results, the consultant, technical management and middle managers carry out an analysis of strengths and weaknesses. The following step is to draw up a plan for the improvement and management of human resources.

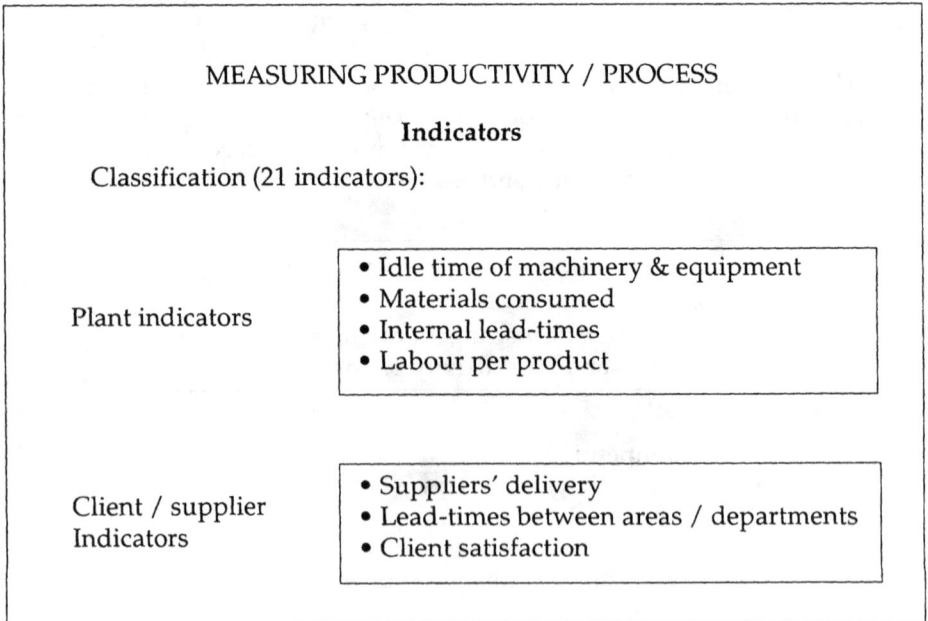

MEASURING PRODUCTIVITY / PROCESS

Indicators

Classification (21 indicators):

Plant indicators	• Idle time of machinery & equipment • Materials consumed • Internal lead-times • Labour per product
Client / supplier Indicators	• Suppliers' delivery • Lead-times between areas / departments • Client satisfaction

---

The measurement of process productivity must:

- contemplate cost, quality, design, flexibility and service to the client;
- adapt to varying circumstances;
- shift indicators when they wear out, or when new market demands appear;
- keep strict parameters or goals;
- emphasise aspects that make a difference for the enterprise on the market.

Employment quality is measured through:

- training delivered
- enriched tasks
- workers' participation
- workers' autonomy
- direct communication to workers
- attitude of superiors toward workers
- system of remuneration by performance
- incorporation to social security
- balance of physical and mental workloads
- safe working conditions
- control of noxious impact on environment
- equal opportunities for women
- no child labour
- job stability
- personnel turnover
- free association

c. Performance of working groups (ProMES)

Opposed to the instruments for measuring economic performance and process, the indicators to be measured through ProMES in working groups are not predetermined. They are jointly developed by management, middle managers and workers on the basis of everyday realities in work performance (Infotep, 2001).

...group performance indicators are an instrument for changing personnel attitudes toward co-operation and informal learning, for solving problems in the work area. It rests on effective communication based on consensus regarding enterprise objectives, performances to be measured, values to be ascribed and follow-up to be adopted...

Before putting ProMES in place, a workshop is held to visualise problems, solutions and the most obvious dysfunctions. Such aspects need prior attention in order to make systematic progress in the enhancement of work processes and conditions.

The indicators of efficiency and quality of the process are measured through effectiveness scores, as well as social aspects like safety, order and cleanliness. Organisational and individual learning come together quite naturally at feedback meetings, without going too deeply. This is learning about coordination and matching criteria on how to perform jobs. On this platform of common understanding – that is constantly evolving – more specific aspects can be considered in depth.

"Many of the problems that come up at these meetings have to do with lack of logistic support (allocation of resources, repair of machinery, procurement of tools, equipment, etc.). Other problems have to do with the lack of skills and abilities of some employees or workers. Training then emerges as a solution. The first specific training activities result from the needs detected by the groups themselves" (Infotep, 2001). It is advisable to materialise training needs and contents through competency profiles or standards, in order to ensure the consistency of training plans. That is the purpose of the fourth instrument.

```
┌─────────────────────────────────┐
│   MEASURING & ENHANCING         │
│   GROUP PERFORMANCE             │
└─────────────────────────────────┘
              ▼
┌─────────────────────────────────┐
│         OBJECTIVES              │
└─────────────────────────────────┘
              ▼
┌─────────────────────────────────┐
│         INDICATORS              │
└─────────────────────────────────┘
              ▼
┌─────────────────────────────────┐
│      EFFECTIVENESS SCORE        │
└─────────────────────────────────┘
              ▼
┌─────────────────────────────────┐
│        MEASUREMENT              │
└─────────────────────────────────┘
              ▼
┌─────────────────────────────────┐
│         DIAGRAMS                │
└─────────────────────────────────┘
              ▼
┌─────────────────────────────────┐
│         FEEDBACK                │
└─────────────────────────────────┘
              ▼
┌─────────────────────────────────┐
│   PROBLEMS, SOLUTIONS,          │
│   AGREEMENTS                    │
└─────────────────────────────────┘
              ▼
┌─────────────────────────────────┐
│         PROGRESS                │
└─────────────────────────────────┘
```

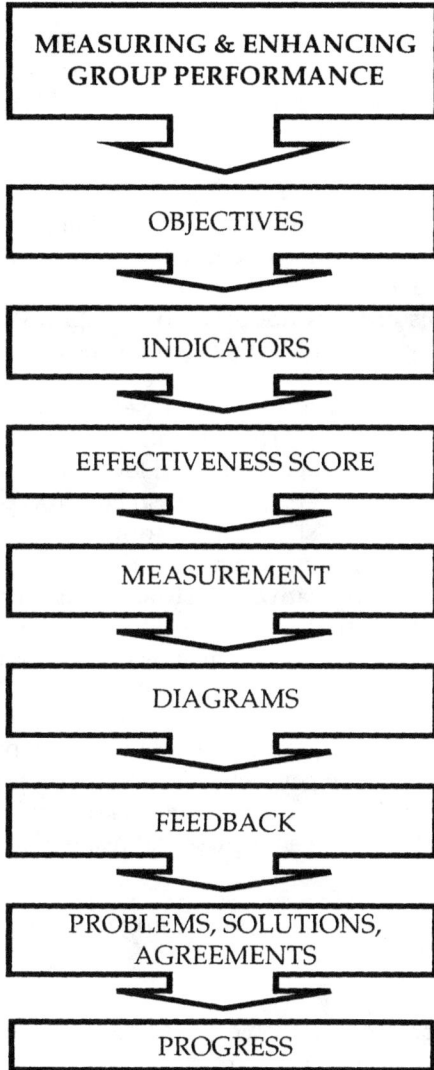

d. Individual performance based on competencies

Individual performance indicators by competencies are even less predetermined than in ProMES, and are jointly built by management, middle managers and a group of expert operatives.

> *...individual performance indicators reflect the person's occupational competencies. They are the result not just of technical abilities and knowledge but also of communication, personal inclination to the job, and the handling of emotions. The reference for measurement is not the work-post but the role...*

The methodology that we followed for building performance indicators is Amod (based on Dacum). This methodology generates a curricular model in which the performances to be demonstrated are ordered by degree of complexity, speciality and depth. This order is not based on a cognitive sequence but on the learning and teaching practices that have worked best in the organisation.

The result is a competencies map organised in modules as defined by the aforementioned technical group. The advantage of this methodology is speed and the participation of different hierarchical levels in the process. The map can be built in one week and workers' self-assessment proceeds immediately after. This is the first step in subject-structured informal training. The second step is the comparison of results of self-assesment with those of an assesment by a supervisor, technician, expert operative or instructor. Construction of an agreement between worker and evaluator on the performance shown *vis-à-vis* the organisation's explicit or implicit standards, is the way in which a learning plan is established minimising differences.

After the plan has been implemented, a certification process may take place in which Infotep validates the competencies acquired by workers at enterprise level. "Infotep acts as facilitator and the enterprise as leading player, as the competency standards pertain to the enterprise and respond to its characteristics and

---

MEASURING INDIVIDUAL PERFORMANCE BY COMPETENCIES

Building steps:
- Enterprise competencies, objectives and strategies
- Area competencies and objectives
- Critical capacities to be taught to area personnel
- Structuring competencies by clusters
- Ordering competencies by degree of complexity and difficulty
- Self-assesment / assesment (5 point scale)
- Certification and registration of certificates by Infotep

interests (…) certification of competencies is formalised through the issuance of certificates in the name of workers, specifying the competencies they master, with the signature of the enterprise certifying committee" (Infotep, 2001).

Certification by Competencies Process and Methodology for Enhancing Productivity

Unstructured informal training occurs in the follow-up of human resources performance indicators. At meetings, workers learn according to the problems they have encountered during the reference period analysed by the indicators. Subjects are not structured, and the knowledge code transferred and/or developed is not formalised.

Amod delivers *structured informal* training. Workers' capacities are developed at the workplace, following the pathway of competencies to be acquired as established on the Amod map. The method encourages workers to engage in a learning dynamic by constantly doing an exercise of self-assessment and assessment by their supervisors or instructors, according to the guidelines laid down by a group of experts on the basis of real working practices and conditions.

The complement of the Amod map are self-training guides, that represent *structured formal* training. Their use requires minimal explanations to workers in the classroom and their evaluation follow-up is formal. Learning codes in the guides are coded and formalised.

To be consistent with a training proposal by competencies and by demand, the training strategy is based on a *file of evidences* that individual candidates have to keep according to the competencies required by their job. This calls for minimal procedures to be followed in the process of assessment and verification of occupational competencies. Assesment by occupational competencies differs from traditional assessment at least in the following aspects: a) it is transparent and based on a given performance standard; b) candidates are the centre of the assessment; it is they, not the evaluators, that keep evidence files for accrediting competencies; c) there is third party referral to ensure the quality and reliability of the assessment process; d) candidates keep and maintain evidence files, not evaluators or verifiers. In this scheme Infotep plays the role of external verifier and is in charge of certifying the enterprise's occupational competency.

The assessment and certification practice based on the Amod map, followed by Infotep, is very similar to the one depicted in the diagram. The diagram is a formalised description of the process (procedure).

TRAINING BY COMPETENCIES MODEL		
Productivity and human resources indicators $\rightarrow$	Developing curriculum by occupational competencies $\rightarrow$	Self-training guides by occupational competencies
$\downarrow$	$\downarrow$	$\downarrow$
Unstructured informal training	Structured informal training	Structured formal training

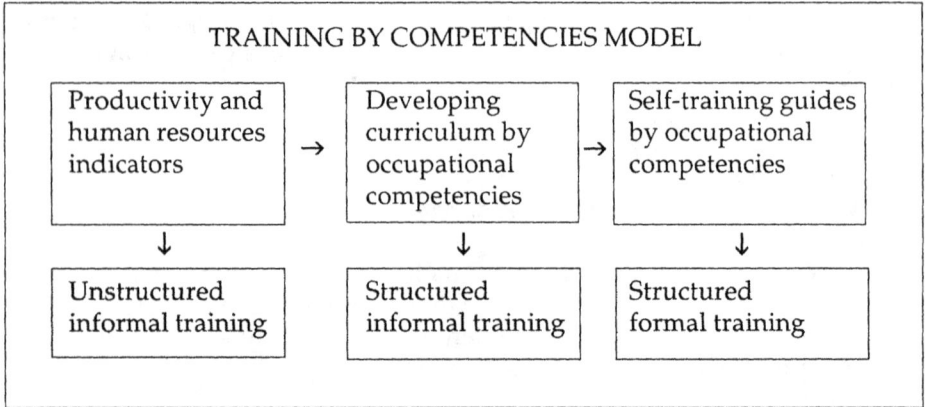

Institutional Application and Learning Pathway

Infotep developed an overall instrument for measuring and enhancing productivity in 1997, in a context wherein the Dominican economy was undergoing a process of trade opening and domestic market deregulation. External circumstances were favourable, with the world economy in full growth and particularly that of the USA: the main trading partner of the Dominican Republic. Despite the fact that the national economy was growing at high rates (5 to 8%) an important structural change was being foreseen, in which Dominican companies would have to adapt to world standards of efficiency, quality and client satisfaction. As in other Latin American countries, few enterprises were prepared for that change and many of them – specially small and medium sized ones – were far from the systems of production, labour and human resources management required to meet new market demands.

Aware of that forthcoming structural change, Infotep considered that its role as main training institution in the country could not be confined to offering initial training to young people joining the labour market and specialisation courses to personnel employed in enterprises. Without leaving aside that line of programming, Infotep envisaged a fundamental proposal for business management, seen as a centre for continuous training requiring new guidelines that could not be generated through the institution's traditional instruments. "…management philosophies, techniques and tools need to be developed enabling enterprises to compete successfully. One answer has been the methodology for enhancing productivity, at a moment when higher levels of efficiency and effectiveness of resources, quality of products and services, client satisfaction and corporate image

ASSESSMENT AND CERTIFICATION MODEL BY OCCUPATIONAL COMPETENCIES

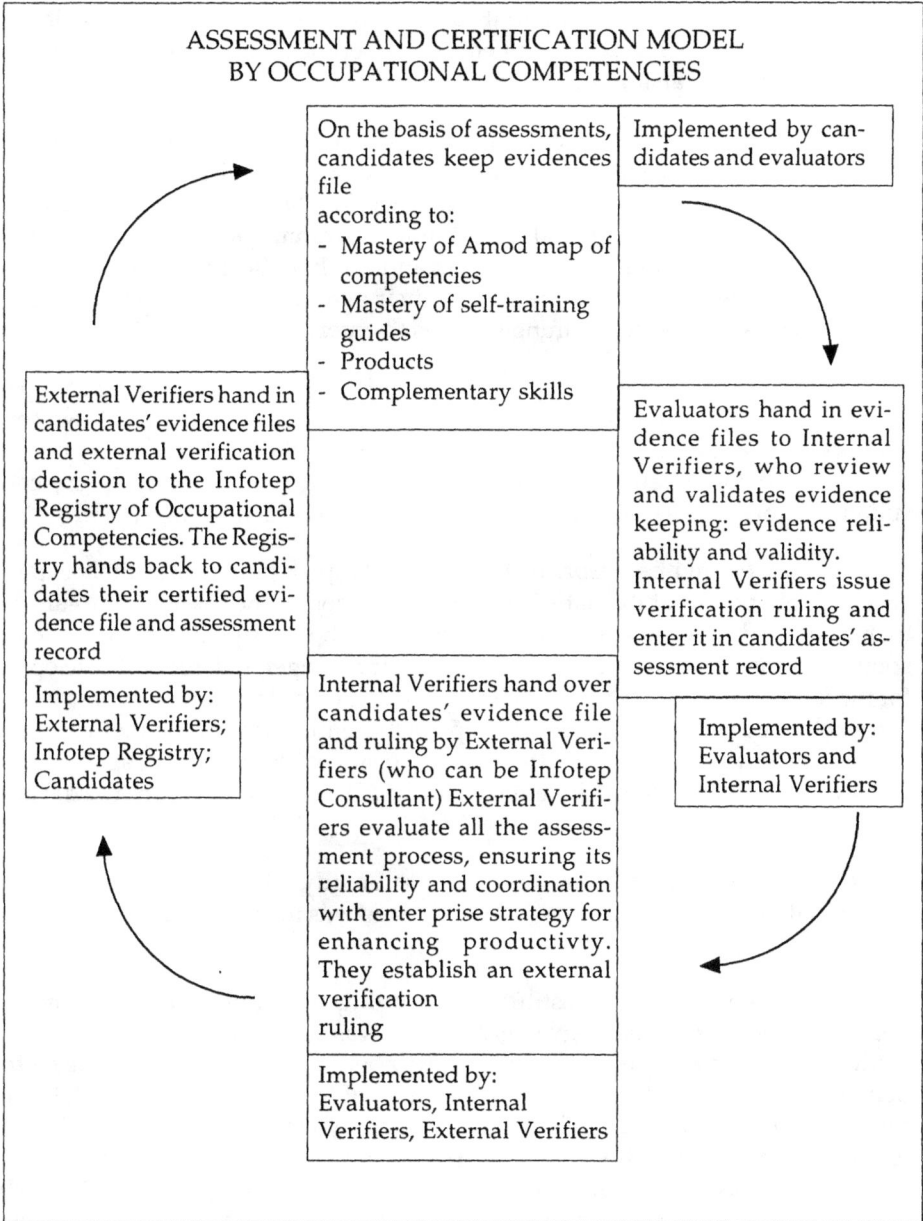

On the basis of assessments, candidates keep evidences file according to: - Mastery of Amod map of competencies - Mastery of self-training guides - Products - Complementary skills	Implemented by candidates and evaluators

External Verifiers hand in candidates' evidence files and external verification decision to the Infotep Registry of Occupational Competencies. The Registry hands back to candidates their certified evidence file and assessment record	Evaluators hand in evidence files to Internal Verifiers, who review and validates evidence keeping: evidence reliability and validity. Internal Verifiers issue verification ruling and enter it in candidates' assessment record
Implemented by: External Verifiers; Infotep Registry; Candidates	

Internal Verifiers hand over candidates' evidence file and ruling by External Verifiers (who can be Infotep Consultant) External Verifiers evaluate all the assessment process, ensuring its reliability and coordination with enter prise strategy for enhancing productivty. They establish an external verification ruling	Implemented by: Evaluators and Internal Verifiers
Implemented by: Evaluators, Internal Verifiers, External Verifiers	

–among other aspects-, are essential for gauging the success of companies. In order to help enhancing competitiveness, Infotep has been applying strategies for measuring and raising productivity since the late 'nineties." (Infotep, 2001a).

Infotep has a consultant area comprised of some forty professionals distributed in its four regional offices. They cover different specialisations: accounting, administration, sociology, psychology, engineering, law, pedagogy. Their functions aim at the following: a. matching Infotep's training offer with the demand of enterprises; b. managing dual training and teachers/technicians' training; c. counselling enterprises on the creation of their own training centres; d. counselling associations that offer training services to enterprises.

Application of the instruments started in May 1997 by coaching the group of consultants in the methodology. The initial proposal was that teams of two consultants each, preferably of complementary specialisations, should carry out pilot experiences in enterprises interested in using the methodology. Every consultant had been assigned at least two experiences in the first stage.

By October, eight enterprises had joined the programme and their experiences were reported at the national productivity conference annually organised by Infotep. This gave rise to new requests from other companies. In order to respond and ensure the firm commitment of their management, the institute opted for the following *rapprochement* mechanism: in the first place, an awareness workshop, followed by a coaching workshop for those in charge of the methodology in the respective enterprises. After these two stages, counselling began *in situ*. Following this plan, some fifty enterprises had been included by mid-2000 and seventy-five in 2001.

A printed manual and an interactive self-study CD were issued for mass dissemination of the methodology. A web page was also created on the Infotep *Internet* site and distance aid was provided.

We may conclude that institutional learning occurred, insofar as time for application of the methodology in enterprises was shortened. Progress was also made in qualitative terms, not only regarding better understanding of the methodology by consultants and the critical aspects of the Dominican context, but in their flexible handling of it. In the beginning they considered that they had to follow all four components. However, two fundamental problems arose in connection with that interpretation: consultants stressed the component with which, by their profession, they were more familiar, and companies did not always accept the development of all four components, especially for economic reasons. In fact, the first problem was particularly serious, as consultants sometimes dealt with instrument components without sufficient knowledge of the topic.

In view of such difficulties, Infotep opted for a more flexible approach, explaining to enterprises the four components and their significance in productivity enhancement strategies. According to the needs of each company, they decided which component to apply and owing to the characteristics of the institution, the tendency was towards components based on workers' group or individual performance.

In time, a problem of organisation and allocation of duties became apparent in the counselling function. Men and women consultants were expected to do so many things, that they could hardly do them all correctly. Besides, some consultants failed to become fully identified with the instruments. Infotep then decided to organise enterprise counselling by specialisations and one them was application of the methodology. Therefore, in all regional offices there are experts in the subject, whose main job is to promote the methodology among companies. By mid-2002, the institute had some 14 methodology specialists at headquarters and in regional offices.

Impact

Quantitative impact

In 2001, Infotep carried out a study of the impact the methodology had had so far both on employers and workers (Infotep, 2001a). We include below some results of the study, together with field observations during the period of application of the methodology.

By mid-2001, the universe of enterprises undergoing some stage of application was 75, with a total employed population of about 10,000. Out of the 75 companies, half were in the initial coaching stage and 29 were already applying the method. By mid-2002, 744 persons had been certified by competencies at enterprise level, by means of the Amod methodology.

Two comments can be made about the application universe. Firstly, the companies belonged to the manufacturing, commerce and services sectors and were large, small and medium-sized. This shows the universal relevance of the methodology, which is no doubt one of its strong points.

The second comment is about intensive or systematic application. In most cases, contact with the methodology has been intermittent, with high and low peaks in measurement and feedback. Few enterprises have incorporated it systematically into their medium term strategy. They seem to have great difficulty in getting over a long-standing, inherited culture of doing business on the spur of the moment, taking advantage of opportunities. Enterprises also seem prey to uncertainty as a result of constant changes in their environment, which prevents them from taking a medium term view.

In most cases, despite temporary application, relevant impacts have occurred and not just momentarily but regarding the process itself. We may wonder if, like Infotep, what we intend is to generate an initial impact motivating enterprises to continue with the methodology, or to achieve a sustained effect in time. The latter is difficult but necessary to verify the hypothesis that the methodology can be sustained in time and continue generating impacts. It has been observed that continuity is not automatic, even in successful cases of application. This has to do with the fact that the methodology involves a change in organisational and managerial culture.

Whenever an unforeseen market event occurs (i.e. a personnel change or a new technology) there is a strong temptation to revert to old paradigms. As we saw with the sugar mills in Mexico, the old culture has an enormous capacity to engulf whatever tries to emerge as a new work culture, oriented toward organisational learning and involving all workers. This does not imply denial of all possibilities of change in that direction, but means that change will not be a straightforward process. There will be an ebb and flow and a variety of approximations for adapting the organisation's work culture to the new contents.

The methodology for measuring and enhancing productivity should be taken as a first step in the development of a system of occupational competencies in the enterprise. The final result of the pilot experience should not be confined to contributing to an individual case of productivity strategy, but to developing a curriculum based on competencies that, through Infotep, may become public property for guiding personnel training in Dominican enterprises, and reorienting the curricula of the occupational workshops managed by the Institution.

In that perspective, rather than a large number of cases, a sufficient level of quality is required to ensure that the curricula derived from the experience may be significant for other enterprises in the same branch. Although cases continue to be individual, a methodology aiming at the development of key competencies can be extrapolated to much broader universes, specially due to the depth case experiences may achieve and to the fact that competencies only apply at the workplace.

Source: ILO/Infotep mission. (Mertens, 1998)

To summarise, the Institution (Infotep) has a methodological proposal that has been tested and has yielded results which give credibility to its messages to the community of workers and employers. Its arguments are no mere allegations. Concrete facts support them, which helps to create an atmosphere promoting the importance of learning in organisations. It all goes to prove that organisational learning, as well as individual participative learning, can be adapted to the context of the Dominican Republic giving good results. It further shows that local enterprises can apply the methodology without needing to qualify as "first world companies". Moreover, at the yearly productivity conferences and other meetings with entrepreneurs that Infotep organises, this "meta-message" has been present underlying reports on application of the methodology, though its effects on the community are difficult to evaluate. Nevertheless, the methodology has become a reference for enterprises wishing to use instruments for improving productivity through human resources. This does not necessarily mean that they will resort to it, but it will serve as a benchmark for any other method they may apply. Consequently, Infotep is offering a pubic domain instrument that contributes to the organisational learning and productivity of Dominican enterprises.

Qualitative impacts

Qualitative impacts refer to intangible aspects that are difficult to measure but have great importance for the organisation and the actors involved, such as inter-personal relations, work environment, communication. They also refer to the actors´ perceptions of impacts which is the subjective part of the process and has been considered essential for learning as it is the driving force that moves personnel.

Although it is preferable for perceptions to be backed by real data, their "objective" value lies in that -in minimal time and with few resources- they convey a picture of the methodology's impacts, through the interpretation of those that have implemented it.

The Infotep study showed interesting results regarding the perceptions of actors (employers, managers, workers) about the impact of the methodology.

Nearly all of them (88.5%) judged it to be beneficial or very beneficial, specially because it enabled them to diagnose the enterprise's situation and look for solutions to the problems identified. Some people also argued that it contributed directly to enhancing productivity which others saw it as beneficial for effectively training personnel (Infotep, 2001a).

133

Two conclusions emerge from the perceptions voiced by entrepreneurs/managers:

The first one is the confirmation that the mere fact of measuring sets off a drive toward improvement. When this happens at the level of upper management, a consolidated impact may be generated, which occurred in the companies that applied economic and process measuring instruments. 75% of them reported improvement in those indicators that have direct effect on consolidated financial results.

The second conclusion is that the methodology influenced productivity, particularly the quality of products and processes, through a different attitude of employees regarding work and the organisation. Just knowing the reasons for decisions, routines, priorities, and feeling the support of upper management, seem to release a converging energy among workers that has a direct effect on the quality and efficiency of processes.

This conclusion stems from the main answers in connection with enhanced quality of products and processes and greater workers' participation in problem solving. The linkup seems obvious, but in the Latin American cultural context that is not necessarily the case in organisations. It requires a "cultural" learning process by managers, middle managers and workers alike (for whom appropriate learning instruments and systems are lacking) capable of imparting training and changing mental attitudes *in situ*. The study shows that the Infotep methodology is a concrete and valid proposal meeting this need in organisations of the Dominican Republic and probably of other countries in the region.

Significant benefits mentioned by some employers as the result of applying the methodology:

- *workers are better organised and have learned to recognise priorities and to communicate for doing their work correctly*
- *we recognised that a change of mindset was required in all the personnel, including administrative workers. The motivation and involvement of employees in enterprise activities has improved*
- *losses by waste and/or rejects in the production process have diminished; personnel management has improved*

In the workers' perspective, the methodology improved the quality of employment in several respects. On the basis of a sample of 59 workers, the Infotep study showed that workers had benefited in the following aspects (ibidem):

a) training of operational personnel and understanding of the job (knowledge of how to perform tasks);

In the six visited enterprises the reactions of interviewed managers and workers to the methodology was very positive. Financial-economic indicators encouraged enterprises to orient their administrative practices in a strategic direction for building indicators and analysing them. In several of them administrative services had been very inadequate. The methodology made them realise that they had to remedy that.

In the case of P., the management commented that financial indicators had helped them to "...be more precise regarding the enterprise's key indicators for strategic planning purposes. They were now better able to decide on initiatives for enhancing productivity". At K., an enterprise that made building blocks, they had never calculated benefits on assets, or unit costs, as they had never had reference costs for an important raw material, the sand that came from a quarry exploited by the same company. After counselling, they were for the first time working out costs and benefits.

Process management indicators helped enterprises to identify weaknesses in their productive process, such as the need to reduce waste (P), delivery time (RD), reprocessing and loss of time in start-up of new machine (K), idle time for maintenance (CF), inadequate operation of equipment cooling system (HN), inventory of processes and jobs redone in paint area (M). As a result of a (self) diagnosis the respective managements took measures for correction/action and improved the indicators in question.

Developing a cluster of human resources indicators had greater impact owing to the highly participative methods used in the process: visualisation to detect improvement needs and opportunities, and ProMES. They are both based on the opinions and viewpoints of workers / employees, which is not something usual in the Dominican society. The main problems identified (and solved) were lack of personnel cooperation with the enterprise's objectives in general, lack of personnel involvement and shortfalls in order and cleanliness (M).

ILO/Infotep mission report (Mertens, 1997).

b)   safety conditions at the enterprise;

c)   workers' involvement in work planning, performance and evaluation;

d)   revaluing work posts and feeling useful;

e)   communication and inter-personal relations with co-workers and management;

f)   individual and group performance;

g)   compensation.

Respondents mentioned other benefits connected with work performance, such as greater ease of execution, motivation for being more efficient and doing better, greater clarity about objectives and weaknesses of the enterprise, and involvement enabling workers to organise their work process and improving their performance.

The validity of the methodology is tested by adding together the perceptions of employers and workers. For instance, they may feel that certain aspects could be improved, specially during the introductory period. They think that the process is sluggish and there is risk of getting stuck in the initial stage and never proceeding to full application. Qualitatively, greater stress should be laid on how to organise work teams and improve communication among them.

For the workers, the shortcomings or gaps in the process may be: a. lack of recognition by management when they do their work well; b. management pays attention to customers, but not to workers; c. not all personnel members are trained in the methodology; d. the training period is too short, it lacks continuity and is ill adapted to the workers' level of schooling (Ibidem).

Counselling remains incomplete: it does not go beyond the launching of the methodology and is seldom followed up, precisely at the moment when the model is taking hold in the organisation and becoming a new work routine.

Example: the workshop for assessing and upgrading human resources is held, indicators and their respective values are identified, but attendance to feedback meetings of workers and middle managers drops off, and the process loses momentum.

Source: ILO/Infotep mission report (Mertens, 1999).

We should now lay down the foundation for a multiplier strategy. It must be based on the conceptualisation and definition of what we are trying to multiply: the entire methodology or its underlying principles? (participation, open-ended training, efficiency and decent work).

The institutional decision needs to be taken as to whether Infotep must be in charge of the multiplier process, or it may include third parties, like private consultants and non-governmental organisations.

Another question is whether the methodology is sufficiently "packaged" and self-contained to be taken up by others without difficulty and applied without the direct support of an Infotep consultant.

Additionally, there is the need to keep the methodology updated with new developments at national and international level, like the Balanced Scoreboard proposal for measuring and improving productivity, and the self-study guides that are being developed with Infotep in the Free Zone of the Dominican Republic.

Source: ILO/Infotep mission report (Mertens, 2001).

Institutional learning: pending agenda

There are fundamentally three challenges facing application of the methodology in forthcoming years. Firstly, the design and deployment of an expansion strategy. Secondly, devising sustainable implementation mechanisms. Thirdly, providing feedback to other Infotep services, specially in the development of curricula for the vocational training workshops that the Institution delivers directly or indirectly.

Regarding the first challenge, it is obvious that Infotep will be unable to reach too many enterprises. To do so, it would have to formulate a strategy involving other partners in the process, with Infotep acting as trainer of internal and external consultants of the enterprises adopting the methodology. It would have to design and/or adapt self-training material for a wider universe of companies. This could be supplemented by promotional and prize-giving activities, like quality awards.

The second challenge is probably more complex. How can we account for the fact that both enterprises and workers should praise the advantages of the methodology, but fail to give it continuity? It would seem that the effort required to sustain it in time –in particular the discipline for systematic measuring and feedback– is not easily incorporated into the existing work and management culture. The same happens with quality systems, but ISO 9000, for instance, is backed by an external auditing system recognised by markets that upholds it in time. Straightforward but significant mechanisms would have to be designed for the methodology to take root in the market and be reflected in the consolidated results of enterprises. Such a mechanism was found for self-training and evaluation guides in the garment industry, as shown below.

A number of critical aspects that must be taken into account when applying the method, and are also terms of reference for a multiplier strategy, were identified at a follow-up seminar with Infotep consultants[17] held in October 2001.

Critical aspects in application of the methodology

- Following up induction workshops offered to entrepreneurs.
- *Coordinating the methodology with the specific needs and strategy of the enterprise, preventing contradictions. An initial diagnosis of the situation is recommended and joint establishment of the project envisaged, focalising objectives and areas addressed.*
- Whenever possible, using financial indicators to obtain an economic picture of the enterprise; ensuring information transparency in this respect and overcoming possible resistances.
- Ensuring and maintaining the support of upper managers and/or informal leaders within the organisation. Keeping management constantly posted on progress made in the application.
- Identifying factors of resistance to the changes in work culture that application of ProMES may imply and working on them, specially the possible reluctance of middle managers to accept additional tasks and/or their wish to conceal a lack of leadership or knowledge.
- Preventing some persons and/or groups from taking over the methodology to wield power within the organisation.
- The complexity of the model should be in keeping with the context and needs of the organisation, especially the measuring capacity of indicators.
- Outlining the competencies' profile of project coordinators on the basis of two main functions: 1. managing ProMES logistics and data processing; 2. keeping up relations with social actors. The competencies required are:

---

17 The seminar was also attended by representatives of enterprises from Mexico and Cuba, where the ProMES and Occupational Competency methodology is being applied.

- Promoting confidence
- Empathy with workers
- Gift of speech
- Knowing how to motivate
- Concentrating on essentials
- Meeting goals
- Orderliness
- Leadership
- Conveying concepts and knowledge
- Acting with common sense
- *Handling computer programmes, especially Excel and Powerpoint*
- Handling problem identification and problem solving techniques (*eg.* Demming)
  - Familiarity with principles of total quality management.
- Appointing assistant for putting model in place, managing model logistics and keeping in contact with key actors (managers, department heads, trade union, workers)
- Formulating a training policy.
- Designing a system for obtaining information and following up commitments.
- *Coaching leaders/facilitators to conduct feedback meetings.*
- Estimating impacts of methodology application by means of a scale, *eg,*
  - Initial and/or progress score
  - Partial and/or periodical score (for a given period)
  - Consistent, wide and constant score
- Making sure that most workers understand the methodology, concepts and parameters used for measuring.
- Timely development of an incentives programme in connection with ProMES results (monetary and non-monetary incentives).
- Maintaining and adapting the methodology in case of unforeseen events, (restructuring operations, market readjustments). In such circumstances, enterprises often give up on the methodology and revert to their former (usually authoritarian) work culture.

As for the third challenge, feedback with the curricular design of technical training workshops, self-training guides and Amod competencies' maps are the "natural" instruments to start reviewing and updating the training workshops and services offered by external collaborating centres. For that purpose, a linkup and follow-up body and culture would have to be developed between both Infotep services.

d. Self-training and Assessment Guides in the Dominican Republic

Application of the Self-training and Assessment Guides began in 2001 in the garment sector at the Santiago free trade zone. Some enterprises of the free zone had previously used the Infotep integral methodology for measuring and enhancing productivity, specially its individual performance (Amod) components. The guides are yet another component (the fifth one) of the integral methodology.

The guides proposal was attractive for the free zone enterprises as it encoded the critical knowledge that had to be shared by their personnel to meet market requirements in connection with costs and quality. It was also attractive because it was an understandable, specific proposal that could easily be implemented by workers with low schooling levels. Additionally, it seemed familiar as it was nearer to the traditional training based on guides or manuals.

Context

Two important aspects should be stressed regarding the context of application of the guides. The first one is institutional. The second one is the development of the Dominican clothes-making industry in the world economy.

Institutionally, one characteristic of the Santiago free zone is that it has a committee of enterprise representatives that manages training funds for employed personnel through an agreement with Infotep. This gives them autonomy in decision-making, close contact with concrete training needs and direct follow-up of

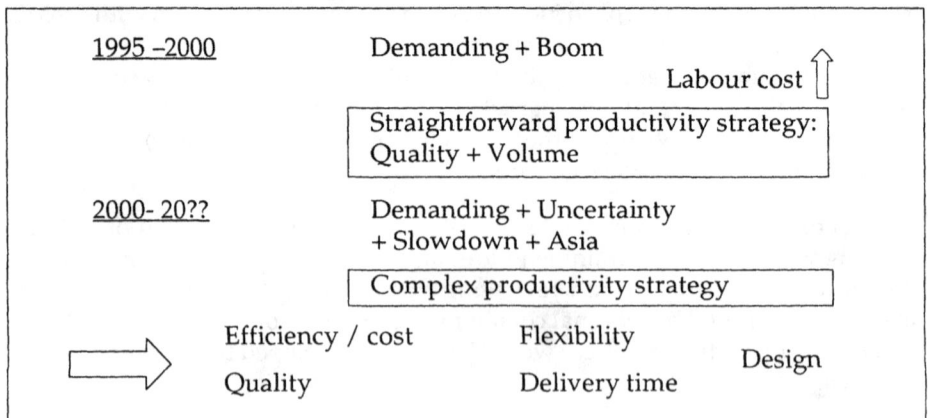

1995 –2000	Demanding + Boom
	Labour cost ⇑
	Straightforward productivity strategy: Quality + Volume
2000- 20??	Demanding + Uncertainty + Slowdown + Asia
	Complex productivity strategy
⇒	Efficiency / cost Flexibility Design
	Quality Delivery time

actions undertaken. Infotep and the committee decided to do a pilot run with the guides in some of the enterprises.

The committee helped the experience to move forwards in two ways. On the one hand, it was empowered to allocate funds to a project with a prestigious institution like Infotep, without going through endless bureaucratic steps. On the other hand, control by the committee and feedback of strategy results into it, led to a plan based on deliverables (products), which obliged consultants to focus their attention on activities.

Another decisive factor has been the positioning of garment enterprises in the overall world economy. The Caribbean basin, Central America and Mexico enjoyed a boom in the garment industry during the 'nineties. They exported mainly to the US market, that was undergoing a period of sustained and high growth. Favoured by low manpower costs, tax advantages and proximity, their strategy was to produce large volumes of the same articles. Assembly work was organised in modules, and quality assured by the presence of inspectors and auditors along production lines.

After 2000, the strategy wore out for several reasons. Labour costs (and generally country costs) had been going up in previous years for macroeconomic causes (stable currencies, greater inflation than in the USA). In addition, the world economy (and in particular that of the USA) went into a period of recession, resulting not only from diminishing demand, but from a downward trend in prices (costs) and delivery times. In times of recession, bringing down prices is the first reaction of companies to make up for the dwindling demand and purchasing power of consumers. For the sake of abating costs, retail chains begin to reduce their inventories but also try make the most of selling opportunities, which forces supplying enterprises to shorten times of delivery.

The predominance of suppliers from South East Asia (China in particular) is constantly increasing. Faced with rising costs, large buying concerns have shifted bulk production to countries where manpower is cheaper than in the Caribbean Basin and the North of Mexico. Here they are now placing special, smaller orders to meet market opportunities that have not been foreseen, or that imply greater risks in sales planning.

The new situation of the garment industry of the Caribbean Basin and North of Mexico in the world economy is moving towards a more complex productivity strategy. At the same time, quality standards are increasingly higher, designs and styles more complicated than in the past, prices (and therefore costs) lower, production flexibility greater and delivery times shorter (for example, 24 days of lead-time for an order including cutting in Florida (USA), assembly in the Dominican Republic and delivery to the USA retailer). This requires a new organisation of work and, above all, better communication, guidance and training of the operatives.

In this context, the proposal of self-training and assesment guides for quality management in the assembly of garments, was well received by the entrepreneurial community of the Santiago free zone. The attractive aspects of the proposal are as follows: a. quality management is focalised on the source, in the man or woman operative; b. guides can be rapidly adapted to the context of each enterprise: c. the learning process is continuous; d. general and specific learning needs can be easily visualised in a coloured chart, which makes it possible to place workers strategically along production lines; e. training costs are low, except for reproduction of the guides; f. use of the guides promotes coordination among workers, supervisors, quality, maintenance and managers.

In response to the complexities of market demands, we did not opt for an exhaustive enumeration and description of all possible performances expected of workers. This would result in an equally complex instrument, difficult to apply and excessively time consuming.

We dealt with complexity at two different levels. Firstly, by making workers understand who were the end consumers of the product, to what lifestyle the assembled garment corresponded, how users satisfied their needs with the garment, which were the critical aspects that consumers underscored. The second level was the need for a comfortable and dignified work environment, self-esteem and personal care to respond to flexibility, style changes, quality, prompt delivery, etc. without a description of all the steps required to achieve them. This occurs gradually through the creation and exchange of tacit knowledge that takes place in a favourable learning context.

The guides have a generic competencies section that covers these aspects and offers a holistic view of specific and operational skills. Generic competencies are a foundation for workers to make decisions and feel confident in taking responsibility for them.

Regarding specific competencies, we managed complexity through focalisation and selection. Instead of analysing and specifying all operations and work posts we selected the five or six most important sub-processes. We applied to each of them a checklist of questions or indications considered to be critical in meeting market requirements, and avoided atomisation into a multiplicity of expected performances.

COMPETENCIES	
Generic	- Client satisfaction - Working under safety standards - Keeping order & cleanliness - Looking after personal and occupational hygiene & health
Specific	- Making rear piece correctly - Making front piece correctly - Making side fastenings correctly - Setting waistband correctly - Doing hems correctly

The list consists of the following questions, whose answers are incorporated *providing that* they represent something specific for the above mentioned competencies. They were devised along the lines of the SCID model:

a. What is critical for the quality of the operation in normal circumstances?
b. What type of decision do you have to make?
c. What information do you have to look up?
d. What problems do you have to solve?
e. What do you have to do in unforeseen situations?
f. What safety aspects do you take into account?
g. What attitudes must you show?
h. What communication do you have to establish?
i. What quality aspects do you have to consider?
j. What are the typical errors to be avoided?
k. What must you do to maintain equipment/facilities?

The training model underlying self-training assessment guides

The training by competencies model in quality management used by operational personnel of enterprises in the Santiago Free Trade Area is based on the following premises:

• The main reference for training are the performances and related knowledge identified in a diagnosis of the problems and strengths of the productive process, quality in particular. The diagnosis is based on knowledge stemming from the experiences and strategic criteria of the best operatives and supervisors, the quality and operations managers and the general management of the enterprises.

- Training is linked to productivity through the following mechanisms:
  i. Encoding good practices, explaining tacit know-how and combining it with available explicit knowledge. Disseminating such knowledge among workers and ensuring that it is implemented. This will promote organisational learning and thus contribute to enhancing productivity.
  ii. Involving operational personnel in the enterprise's objectives, channelling the human energy of the organisation into a common, shared direction.
  iii. Systematically following up personnel training plans, connecting them with problems and opportunities for improving productivity.
  iv. Modifying the supervisory function, specially the role of supervisors, turning them into facilitators and managers of organisational learning.
  v. Encouraging and following up proposals and suggestions by personnel regarding the production process and the organisation of work.
  vi. Monitoring productivity indicators in the respective areas or departments and relating them to the training required.

- Assessment of performance and related knowledge is the basis for training. Training is guided by constant self-assessment and the evaluation of critical aspects of quality management in relation to the tasks of workers.

- Training is not an isolated or discrete event but a ongoing process, managed and measured through periodic assessments of the application of competencies that are considered to have a key or critical value. An annual cycle of at least three evaluations is recommended, establishing individual plans of training activities that each worker must complete before the following assesment. Certification of the workers' competencies may be renewed after every cycle, for example, for the years 2002, 2003, 2004, etc.

- The training and assessment instrument is flexible and can be adapted to the context of each enterprise, its current productivity and competitiveness. Nonetheless, the use of a common structure is recommended for different companies of the same economic subsector so as to create a "scale economy" but with individual adjustments (similar to what is known as "mass customisation", i.e. collective compliance with the requirements of customers). This makes it possible to develop a speedy response *(express learning)* with *ad hoc* contents according to the needs of each company.

- Reference is made to good practices, but also to common errors that need to be avoided. Not only technical subjects are discussed but also matters relative to communication, attitudes and emotions, that a socially responsible enterprise is supposed to look after. Presentation of the material is fundamentally graphic, with the support of digital photos of work areas and details of the various operations. Teaching involves exercises and instructions through which workers assimilate knowledge by answering questions and doing assignments based on the technical information included in the manuals themselves.

- Training has a self-directive or self-learning component that consists of active participation of students (workers) in the process. This allows for personalised progress in learning, ascribing responsibility for it to each individual. The enterprise must provide the wherewithal (materials, premises, time schedule, support personnel). This does not preclude use of the classroom, but turns it into a meeting place for the different groups of operatives to share their knowledge, with the assistance of supervisors and programme coordinators. Traditional instructors are not used. A space for analysis and reflection is promoted between workers, supervisors and some experts (in quality management, for instance). Performance evaluation occurs at the workplace and is one more stage of on-the-job training. It is the most important component of the training process as it represents its materialisation into the productive process.

- Learning is effective and of low cost because it focuses training on those competencies and persons that fall short of expected performance standards, instead of extending it to all workers and covering all competencies identified.

- The role of TVET institutes in supporting training at enterprises is no longer just supplying courses. They become consultants on the design and delivery of training as an integral part of the respective organisations' strategic management. This enables institutions to act as observatories of the new competencies that emerge in the productive realm, and translate them into curricula for the initial or basic training courses they offer.

Application and Institutional Learning Pathways

Start-up was slightly different from that of the integral methodology for measuring and enhancing productivity. Instead of holding a training workshop for facilitators, we began with a coaching scheme. Two enterprises were chosen to take part in the project: a large and modern concern (approximately 7 thousand persons), and a medium, less modern company (approximately 500 persons). The guides were gradually developed with them. Reflection meetings on the steps being taken were held from time to time with the Infotep experts of the North Regional Office who were in charge of the project. In those opportunities, doubts were clarified and the methodology was fine-tuned.

At the enterprises, the project was submitted to executive managers who were asked to appoint an internal coordinator to manage it within the organisation. Two meetings were held at each enterprise with expert line personnel, supervisors, quality managers and plant managers, in order to adapt the guides to the needs and specifications of each plant.

The two women coordinators were coached to draw up the guides along the lines of the basic model adopted. In ten days' time they had made enough progress to continue unaided for another three weeks, completing the guides with no further external coaching and making them available for a trial run.

The pathway outlined from then on was as follows: starting a pilot experience with a module of some 30-35 persons, evaluating it and then extending the model to other modules. We reckoned that in six months' time about six modules could be incorporated in each enterprise. However, reality proved otherwise.

The fact of having the guides ready and very enthusiastic coordinators does not mean that enterprises can automatically launch and multiply the process of application. They think it is all very nice and like having a manual tailored to their needs but an outside stimulus is required to trigger and maintain the application process.

Such was the case of the two enterprises in our pilot experience. They had their guides ready for several months but, for a number of reasons, lacked the initiative to use them. Practical introduction of the guides required further follow-up and coaching. This consisted of three follow-up and feedback sessions in each enterprise, to secure the support and involvement of directors and managers.

The result was an alignment of all processes connected with application of the methodology (objectives of the enterprise and objectives of the guide), clarification of the view underlying the guide, the commitment of managers to the project and the setting of short and medium term goals (one month and four months, respectively).

Despite the progress made by follow-up and coaching, diagnosis was not very encouraging in either of the two cases. Managers and middle managers were willing enough, but the project was competing for time and attention with many other issues stemming from the structural transformation of the market, for which these companies had not yet found an answer.

The situation was paradoxical. On the one hand, the guides met the needs of the enterprises for managing quality at the source and keeping their personnel focused on their objectives. On the other hand, changes of context demanded new work procedures and management styles that the enterprises were learning along the road. Faced with uncertainty, their usual reaction was to fall back on old practices of personnel management, because "firstly, we must redesign processes".

DIAGNOSIS: WEAKNESSES, ENTERPRISE 1

- **Strategic positioning of project:**

There was confusion as to whether personnel strategy should be to bring down costs through wages, by reducing dependence on specialised workers (eg. waistband makers), or to reduce labour costs through an enhancement of personnel productivity. If a wage reduction strategy was adopted, interest in application of the guides was likely to decline.

- **Leadership in project management:**

Involvement of the company's directors in the project has been scarce, including the general manager of the factory. Support of the executive management is still unclear.

There are no common criteria among upper and middle managers about the strategy to be followed or the command structure. This hinders implementation of the project, specially the need of resources for it.

- **Resources for the Project:**

Financial support is scarce. It took months to reproduce the guides, which delayed start-up. Workers have not been given time in their schedule to analyse the guides collectively, and the coordinator has been assigned a multiplicity of other tasks.

Under such circumstances, the goodwill of managers is not enough to start off a process of continuous learning. in a context of uncertainty such as the one being experienced by the Dominican garment industry, a sufficiently strong external incentive or pressure is required for middle and upper managers to become really committed to the process.

The operational personnel has shown a good deal of interest and enthusiasm in "working" the guides. But this vanishes rapidly if there is no follow-up or commitment by management.

In the subsequent four months, application of the methodology came up against some difficulties and decisions that, seen from outside the enterprises, seem quite irrational.

At Enterprise 1 there was a major managerial reshuffle, among other things because a new shareholder joined the company and went on the board of directors. Various middle managers were demoted, including the coordinator of the guide. Nevertheless, the guide was applied in one module and quality and efficiency results went up steadily during four weeks. Instead of going on with that module and starting with a new one, they broke up the team that had been work-

---

DIAGNOSIS: WEAKNESSES, ENTERPRISE 2

- **Strategic positioning of project:**
The module that started with the guide was assigned a complicated garment to manufacture, which caused a lot of rework and loss of time. Other modules have to change styles constantly, which impairs efficiency as there is no clear strategy for organising work with the flexibility the market demands. The guides run the risk of losing priority in view of the many contingencies of the process.

- **Leadership in project management:**
Management of the project is in the hands of a single person. Although this person has the backing of the management, support of Infotep technicians is required for leadership purposes.

- **Resources for the project:**
The premises are inadequate for personnel meetings . Workers do not have where to put their belongings, including the guides, and many keep them in their workplaces for lack of personal lockers

---

ing on the guide and redistributed its members among other areas that were in trouble. This was not a well thought out action in line with a strategy, but a reaction to the moment of desperation the company is undergoing in its search for answers to new market demands.

It was not easy to uphold application of the guide in the midst of such a storm of changes. We developed a new strategy with the management, with a commitment to reinitiate application in two modules simultaneously.

Enterprise 2 also underwent a turmoil of changes in management and supervision, perhaps worse than that of Enterprise 1. Here the advantage was that the project coordinator (another woman) remained, so that the continuity of learning was not lost. However, the module where application had started went into crisis as the quality and efficiency goals were not achieved. The organisation is also frantically trying to find flexibility of production, faced with a diversity of designs and styles with varying degrees of complexity. Lack of planning, communication and coordination are evident.

The use of the guides could contribute to more fluent communication between operational and directive personnel and better work coordination. But here again, it was easier to relapse into old habits of contradictory orders without clarifying explanations, which resulted in rework, bad quality and low efficiency.

An agreement was reached with the new management for resuming application of the guide. Infotep will have to follow up this decision. A learning process has already taken place with the guides; the test will be whether it can survive in adverse conditions.

The experiences with these two enterprises led the Infotep team of consultants to some conclusions. For instance, application of the guides in a context of change and dysfunctional situations previously requires a shared diagnosis among all those involved about what is being pursued and what obstacles have to be overcome for making progress. They considered that ProMES was a suitable instrument for this, for it involved workers and created a favourable environment to proceed with application of the guide.

This period of reflection and learning coincided with a request from a casual wear trader for application of the guide in the eleven small and medium-size *maquila* enterprises with which they had subcontracts. They had seen the guide at Enterprise 2 (one of their eleven subcontractors) where it was first tried out. Infotep and the trader agreed that application of the guide should be part of the system of scores that they ascribed to subcontractors for awarding them contracts.

The challenge for Infotep was to show that is was possible to start by the accelerated stage of application of the methodology. Instead of following up two enterprises, now there were eleven, and besides the guides, ProMES would also be used.

Consequently, follow-up included the eleven enterprises dependent on the trader, who had contracts with the large chains of self-service retailers in the USA.

Main lessons learned in the first stage of application of training and evaluation guides:

- the guides' design is aimed at self-directed group or individual learning;
- group work with the guides enables workers to share experiences and knowledge, promoting learning among personnel doing the same job;
- a pilot experience should be consolidated initially, extending it to other areas once it has proved to be functional;
- the more hierarchical levels are involved in the process, the greater will be the support and impact of the guides;
- the project management structure (enterprise coordinator, consultant assigned to the case, project coordinator and external consultant) balance and consolidate the process;
- simultaneous application in two companies of different organisational level enables us to compare practical improvements and learn from respective advances;
- workers' certification after three evaluations can lead to a longer training process, and also means a temporary halt for the personnel involved;
- application of the guides brings out a new profile for supervisors, a resource enterprises need very much nowadays but are generally unable to generate;
- new competencies are detected in enterprises during the process of application. The consultant department, in its capacity of observatory, must communicate them to the Institution's technical training division;
- productivity can only be directly correlated with training action by simultaneously acting on other factors, like technology.

Advances made during four months of application of the guide were remarkable. The new trading agreement and consistent work by the consultants – who came together as a true team-, led to the following results in the initial application of the enlarged methodology:

Quantitative progress:

The scheme started by applying the productivity measurement system (ProMES) in one or two modules at each enterprise. The self-assesment/assesment "express guide" in quality management was adapted to the context of each company. The stage of application of the guides with the personnel of modules already utilising ProMES is about to begin. The universe of workers employed in the enterprises participating in the pilot run is about 8,000.

Qualitative progress:

During the period March-July 2002, qualitative progress in use of the methodology involved:

-   Uniformity of criteria among consultants in charge of introducing the methodology. Their work was focalised through the involvement and leadership of the management. Teamwork by motivated personnel in pursuit of objectives laid out.
-   The team of consultants mastered the ProMES and "express guides" methodologies. Proof of this is that they extended them to nine enterprises and adapted the guide in three weeks. This fulfilled the objective of developing a training

---

Plan for including other enterprises of the Santiago Free Zone that work as subcontractors to main trader:

- starting the pilot stage in each enterprise by applying ProMES in one module;
- at the same time, adapting the self-training and evaluation guides to each enterprise and using them in combination with ProMES in the same module;
- implementing the second stage, i.e. partial extension of ProMES and guides to other modules;
- certification of the personnel involved towards the end of 2002.

---

instrument for the enterprises in a short time, which was aided by the fact that they all belonged to the same sub-branch of the garment industry.

- Application of the productivity measurement (ProMES) methodology immediately before the guides was beneficial. It made it possible to identify the main dysfunctions in the area, creating a favourable environment for the structured learning with the guides to have its expected impact.
- The decision of extending the pilot experience to nine enterprises instead of concentrating on the two initial ones was correct. Those two companies underwent managerial restructuring processes, which delayed advance in application of the methodology. In the meantime, the team of consultants got ahead with the other enterprises of the garment industry that supplied the same trader.
- It was also right to deal with companies working for the same wholesaler; this was an element that pressured them into accepting the methodology. It also enabled them to standardise efficiency criteria and exchange good practices. It further sustained incorporation of small and medium enterprises of the Free Zone into the world economy.
- The guides had good acceptance. Enterprises like to have a tangible instrument, a product, even though they may not apply it afterwards.
- The methodology promoted the image and credibility of Infotep consultant services among enterprises. Demand for counselling on use of the methodology has exceeded by far Infotep's capacity. The technical / professional merits of Infotep consultants are acknowledged in entrepreneurial circles.
- Several companies where the methodology is being applied also take part in another Infotep programme called "la escuelita" (the little school). Enterprises provide space and machinery to train inexperienced persons with an instructor paid by the Infotep Free Zone Project. An initial step for integrating productivity and occupational competencies' methodology with Infotep vocational training system is to link up the "escuelita" with the introduction of methodology (at ProMES feedback meetings, during application of the guides).

Areas of opportunity identified for further extending application were as follows:

- Providing further training in basic computer skills for consultants for application of the methodology;
- Ensuring that enterprises process and record graphically ProMES results by modules and by indicators. Such graphs should be made visible to opera-

tives in work areas (for instance with showcases);

- Including in ProMES the social indicators used by the enterprise (absenteeism, order and cleanliness, safety and accidents);

- Linking up ProMES with the 5Ss methodology;

- Establishing and applying a standard follow-up format for commitments that may arise at feedback boards;

- Introducing costs analysis into the methodology to guide decision making. Use of a *Balanced Scorecard* may help to visualise and follow up the enterprise's strategy;

- Updating consultants on new trends in technology and organisation of the clothes-making industry at international level. Suggestions: registering with specialised Internet websites and holding internal seminars with specialised personnel of the Santiago industry (for example, asking a leading enterprise or business person to give their views on work organisation in the branch);

- Making someone in the enterprise responsible for the methodology, so that the Infotep consultants do not have to act as executing agents;

- Promoting motivational activities among employees: get-togethers, promotional material (leaflets, T-shirts, caps, banners); half-yearly awards (raffles, bonuses);

- Drafting a trainers/evaluators' guide by competencies for supervisors, expert workers and external consultants, in order to have a multiplier effect within and without the enterprise. Infotep will act as trainers' trainer, a process that includes certification of trainers/evaluators and verifiers;

- Providing training, documentation and experiences for trainers in pedagogic techniques facilitating application of the guides and giving depth to ProMES feedback boards;

- Training consultants, internal coordinators and facilitators (trainers/evaluators) in problem-solving techniques and analysis;

- Establishing a standard format to document cases (If there are difficulties in documentation, a format may help to structure it);

- Establishing with enterprises that internal coordinators of the methodology should submit periodical executive reports on application progress, also with a standard format if they wish. This helps enterprises to keep control of the process, reporting advances and obstacles to directors for decision making;

- Feeding back results (guides, indicators, follow-up commitments) to Infotep workshop instructors and collaborating centres;

- Making the project visible by means of video recordings of experiences, showcases of instruments utilised, website;

- Defining homologation criteria for the report on application of the methodology, in accordance with administrative formats used by Infotep (coursehours, number of persons trained, certified hours vs. performance);
- Providing special follow-up to cases that started with the methodology and are currently being restructured;
- Systematically involving the wholesale trader into the process, to coordinate their productivity and quality strategies with the methodology, secure their material support and induce them to put pressure on their *maquila* subcontracting enterprises for commitment to the methodology. They can help specially in the reproduction of the guides, in persuading enterprises to provide meeting places, in supplying promotion material (*eg.* a poster on critical quality points).

Progress was made not only in the application process. Concrete improvements also took place within the enterprises, specially in those that had advanced further in the use of the methodology at the cut-off date.

This experience has been localised in the North Regional Office of Infotep. It has not yet expanded to other regional offices. A third stage will have to be designed, extending application to enterprises where the external consultants will not be the same that started using the guides. The idea is that Infotep should devise and offer a training "course" based on competencies for facilitators of the methodology. It would be based on a self-training and evaluation manual for guide facilitation, comprising knowledge and performances. This guarantees that the certification of facilitators by Infotep goes through a process of real application of the guide, hand in hand with the expansion of the proposal.

QUALITY AND PRODUCTIVITY OBJECTIVES

- Bringing faults % in modules down from 20% to 2% at end of Project
  - Faults % = Vol. Faults / Vol. Sample

- Stabilising daily production in 1,000 trousers, and raising minimum production to 1,100 trousers a day by end of Project

- Current situation: we are 8% down, as compared with 15% or 20% in other modules

High Grade

RESULTS

- Standardising quality concepts

- Integrating workers into teams

- Awareness of importance of feedback

- Incentives for taking initiatives (knowing operations cluster)

- Using guide as manual for training new workers and retraining old ones

- Higher motivation

- Facilitating work of supervisors and quality controllers

High Grade

5

EFFECTS ON LINK-UP STRATEGIES BETWEEN TVET INSTITUTES AND ORGANISATIONS

The ProMES methodology and self-training and assesment guides break away from the traditional paradigm of Technical Vocational Education and Training (TVET) Institutions which consists of offering courses for the operational and supervisory personnel of organisations. That activity continues to be valid as a contribution to the occupational development of persons. What the methodologies here presented intend to do is to bridge the gap between school and work, in a way that goes beyond deriving curricula from productive practices and doing exercises in the courses.

The first question that TVET Institutes have to answer is whether they consider that their role is to train individuals or collective groups, or a combination of both. If TVET institutions think that their role is to train individuals, and that it is up to organisations to incorporate them into their occupational systems, they will not have much use for the methodologies described here.

On the contrary, if TVET bodies consider that their role is also to promote learning in collective groups (organisations), guiding them in the constant enhancement of productivity and working conditions, then ongoing and all-inclusive learning methodologies should be part of their operational strategies. This does not mean that they should take over management of the organisations' training activities. There is an area of shared responsibility in these methodologies but it must be made clear from the start that the organisations themselves, not the TVET Institutes, are responsible for the continuous learning process.

Regarding TVET institutions that take this view, what are the effects of application of ProMES and self-training/evaluation guides methodologies on their strategies for linking up with enterprises and organisations? On the basis of our experiences in Mexico and the Dominican Republic, we have identified the following:

a. Nature of link-up

The idea is that organisations should apply ongoing and all-inclusive training models aimed at the constant enhancement of productivity and working conditions. TVET institutions will provide the necessary support for developing the most appropriate proposal.

This implies that TVET bodies must develop a technical capacity for building such training models, undergoing an institutional learning process from theory and concept to practice. Like any other learning process, it requires a strategy for gauging progress through periodical training evaluations.

This view opens up a wide range of fields of action for TVET institutes, which involves a risk of losing and scattering impacts. It is essential therefore to demarcate the scope of activities. The management of human resources in the organisation concerned is a first demarcation, but even there the field is too wide. Focalisation might start by an instrument enabling workers to contribute – through continuous learning – to the constant improvement of productivity and working conditions.

b. Impact planning

The impact sought by TVET institutes will not be reflected in the number of cases, which will never be enough. The impact achieved will lie in the significance of the application. The learning to be disseminated in the corporate and trade union communities should be encoded on the basis of a trial run. Encoding serves to adapt the methodology to the national or regional context, and also permits to "package" it for others to use with adequate external counselling. It can also be an input for feedback into the design of curricula for the formal courses of TVET institutes.

Just as in the management of traditional courses, TVET bodies can train, evaluate and certify others in the use of the methodology. This is a more deliberate way of generating impacts than mere dissemination.

c. The role or organisations/enterprises

Organisations have traditionally played a passive role in linking up with TVET institutions, at best confining themselves to a diagnosis of their training needs. They have concerned themselves with administrative details (time schedule of courses, costs, location, participants) but very little with actual contents. For that they have relied on TVET institutes.

In the case of ProMES and the guides, the organisations' management has to become involved in the project and integrate it into its strategy and everyday practice. To the extent that even the project leader should not belong to the human resources division but to the operations area, as learning takes place in there. This means that the operations division must be envisaged not just as executor of predetermined routines but also as generator of a continuous learning process. From a cultural point of view this is a radical change, for it implies accepting that there are many "loose ends" in management, and there are always opportunities for performing operations in a better way. It requires a different style of leadership, open to participation and experimentation by the personnel.

d. Application pathway

Application of the methodology is not a uniform process. Consistency with the main purpose should be kept, that is the ongoing, all-inclusive learning both of individuals and the organisation. The goal is not generating other identical applications. Each case is just an instance of how the purpose can be achieved, but is open to adaptation to the needs of other organisations. When they have few procedures and systems of work management and communication, organisations can take up the methodology with all its components. However, if they are well structured and have a culture in planning and systems, they generally pick those components that are a complement to what they already have and function adequately for them.

This means that TVET institutions must approach each case with an open mind, not imposing the methodology but presenting it as an example. This calls for a cultural change in the training institutions themselves, whose members do not always take an attitude of learning with others. They usually manage methodologies in an orthodox and rigid manner, in the belief that they are complying with their function. When there are subsidies, enterprises may accept commitments with training institutions simply because they are free of charge. The veritable acid test occurs when enterprises have to finance the application, external counselling included. TVET bodies then have to strive in that direction, persuading them to bear the costs.

e. The role of TVET institutes in training activities

The methodology does not foresee that training institutions should plan, organise, implement and evaluate training activities. Their role is to provide coaching in the principles of the methodology without following a rigid scheme. It is a mistake for them to stop at the diagnostic stage not suggesting solutions, or not to go along with the solutions proposed. Another mistake is to impose pre-established curricula or competency standards: the essence of this methodology is that each organisation should do its own homework, otherwise it will not succeed.

TVET institutions have to train internal coordinators and facilitators at enterprises, and external consultants not belonging to them (to the institutions). Training takes place through products or deliverables: profiles, manuals, knowledge and performance evaluation instruments, manuals of procedures, systems managing the process, training guides for internal facilitators and evaluators.

This faces training institutions with a consultant's profile completely different from that of persons who have traditionally delivered courses at enterprises. These new experts must have an updated view of business, markets and organisational development. They must also have sufficient analytical capacity to put together fragments of tacit and explicit knowledge into a consistent plan and turn it into a training guide. They must have a gift for communicating easily with high management and workers alike, keep an open mind to different viewpoints and at the same time be persevering enough to meet agreed goals. They should possess a power of synthesis, encouraging project participants to help with their talents and capacities in the process of application. Another key competency they require is to be systematic and orderly, without verging on insensitivity in moments of decision, which will always appear.

The above are some of the key competencies of TVET consultants responsible for promoting the methodology. Implementing it requires a cultural transformation inside training bodies, for which they need to adopt an individual and collective learning strategy. In the case of the Dominican Republic, at the Infotep North Regional Office, when the team of consultants managed to set off a systematic and focalised process of reflection and learning, results flourished quite naturally and goals were gradually met without conflict. The image the institution had among enterprises improved, and demand for consultant services on the methodology grew.

Revamping a vocational training institute in this direction is difficult and not devoid of troubles. Some TVET institutions in Latin America have managed to embark upon this course. However, when managers and directors are overly concerned with political visibility, they are unlikely to feel inclined to lead a process of change of this kind.

f. Some requirements TVET institutions must fulfil for the ProMES methodology and self-training and assessment guides proposal to succeed

a. Total support of the institutions' directors, placing the methodology at the centre of consultant services to enterprises and organisations.

b. Mastery of the technology by core members of the institute, which guarantees internal consistency (a methodology manual can be a sample of this).

c. Development of a uniform language among consultants, permitting to evaluate them clearly and objectively according to their proven capacity,

d. Clear-cut format by blocks or modules, facilitating communication with enterprise managers, and visualising with them a systematic and understandable work proposal to tackle a complex subject like productivity and occupational competency.

e. Correct promotional strategy for approaching employers and workers through promotion seminars and other means.

f. Flexible application: the method has to be adapted to the needs of enterprises and the capacity of consultants.

g. A view of integral training underpinning the methodology. This leads to relevant answers to problems or opportunities during application in different organisations.

h. Good response capability in the TVET institution, and continuity in its relations with organisations through the services it offers.

i. Ensuring immediate impacts in organisations.

j. Using an exponential expansion strategy whenever the methodology is applied.

k. Application in small, medium-sized and large enterprises. Lessons learned in large enterprises can be transferred to small and medium ones, and vice versa.

l. Capability by the TVET institute for recording and managing certificates.

g. The role of organisations in training activities

Organisations are mainly responsible for the success of the proposal and must adapt it to their needs. As happens with other projects, the proposal is liable to suffer from resistance to change or from the impact of market ups and downs. As it has come to stay in the organisation, we must bear in mind that it has to go through a number of stages during application: start-up with a pilot experience, expansion and maturity, possible reversal due to relapse into meaningless routines as a reaction to an innovative process.

In the current context, there are two great threats in organisations hampering the introduction of a methodology of this kind. The first one is the accelerated volatility that virtual economies are infusing into management: from the very beginning of the process, under the influence of the latest novelty or theory, some anxious participants will be looking for an alternative project. The second threat is the constant change of upper and middle managers in organisations that have failed to find a solution to their changing surroundings and expect to do so by shuffling their personnel around.

Both threats must be taken into account for achieving dynamic planning and avoiding a process of constant modifications in managing the project. In the cases described here, the methodology – and ProMES in particular – have proved to be quite impervious to internal and external onslaughts. But there are limits, and organisations should be aware of what stage of application of the methodology they are at, and what their own metamorphosis has been.

Probably the most difficult thing for organisations to accept is that they themselves are responsible for the training, especially that of the operatives. This does not mean that all training activities are in the hands of internal personnel, but they are responsible for managing the continuous learning process. This is not to be left to others (through subcontracts or outsourcing) because it is the very heart of productivity management, the core of dynamic competitive advantage. Unfortunately, forced by the need to abate costs in the short term, many organisations yield to the temptation of cutting back on non-essentials, anything that is not required for immediate survival.

This also conceals deeper misgivings, like a fear of new styles of leadership, the need to acquire new competencies without knowing beforehand if they will be able to master them. Moreover, by adding confusion and constant changes of objectives, the motivation their personnel may have to get actively involved in the project vanishes altogether.

A *sine qua non* condition for the methodology to take hold is to build and maintain firm leadership in managing the project and outside pressures may sometimes contribute to this (*eg.* clients' requirements, compliance with ISO quality standards). We saw it at a sugar mill in Mexico, where the methodology helped to get workers involved in everyday management, or in the case of the wholesale garment trader in the Dominican Republic, that included the use of the methodology in its contractual conditions.

h. Costs management

Application of the methodology implies costs, which are not constant along time. During the initial stage costs are high because counselling is needed to adapt the model to the characteristics of the enterprise in question, and to train internal coordinators and facilitators. Costs go down as the organisation appropriates the methodology and the model becomes consolidated. In the case of the guides, initial costs are higher than for ProMES as their design and edition take time.

Another peak in costs occurs when the guides have to be reproduced and space has to be provided for persons to meet. This is even more critical when there are high rates of personnel turnover.

How can TVET institutions manage costs? Traditionally, they have utilised cost per hour of instruction plus support material and teaching aids. The system is no longer valid for application of this methodology. If emphasis lies on self-training with the assistance of facilitators, costs are concentrated at both ends of the process: a. in the drafting and reproduction of the guides, and b. in the process of evaluation/feedback by each participant.

Terms of reference for the link-up between the TVET institution and the organisation vary according to the parts of the methodology to be applied. The training institution and the organisation must jointly determine what products are to be considered. One organisation may want first to obtain a competencies' profile, another may wish to apply self-training/assessment guides immediately, a third one to start off with ProMES. As opposed to traditional training, where the cost of inputs was taken into account, in this methodology costs are related to results or deliverables (products).

Costs management is in no way obvious, for many deliverables depend on the degree of personnel involvement in the project pathway. It would be too demanding to work only on deliverables when not all aspects of the process are under control. We may consider a halfway alternative, like paying for a number of hours of programmed consultant services, with the commitment of reaching certain levels of deliverables for each specified stage.

TVET institutes can play an important role in the reproduction of the guides, the cost of which will go down drastically with electronic resources. Training institutions can negotiate reproduction packages for several enterprises at a time, and get better prices from suppliers. All the same, it is an investment that enterprises are not accustomed to, which may sometimes cause disproportionate and irrational reactions by management. That is the moment when TVET institutions can submit arguments justifying the investment and suggest alternative solutions.

In brief, training institutions will have to modify their usual schemes of allocating resources and drawing up budgets that are no longer in consonance with the needs stemming from ongoing learning.

The above consequences are not an exhaustive list and there are no doubt many more. The ones we included were only sketchily dealt with, and their importance go beyond what we have managed to describe. However, this may help in the process of reorientation of TVET institutions, making them more proactive to the learning processes required to achieve productivity and sustainable employment quality.

6
CONCLUSIONS

This study has shown that ongoing, all-inclusive learning methodologies and instruments aiming at enhanced productivity and working conditions can be applied in Latin American organisations. Flexibility, adaptability, systematic management and a structure based on competencies have made such training processes functional and have yielded concrete and measurable results.

The two methodologies presented, ProMES and Self –Training/assessment Guides, are mutually complementary and have certain advantages and disadvantages. The first method can be put in place immediately, the second one requires a process of adaptation before application. While in the former training is extensive and refers to coordination at work and the solving of direct problems, in the latter learning is deeper and involves the understanding of phenomena of the work process. This helps individuals to develop sounder mental make-ups and contribute to collective learning through the interaction of tacit and explicit knowledge at higher levels.

The two methodologies were applied in modern organisations and in backward ones, in small and large enterprises, which bears witness to the universality of their proposal. This makes them attractive for TVET institutions of the region, that need effective methods that can be applied in different contexts. Scale economies can be generated and may bring down costs for mass application.

We may conclude that a proven methodological proposal of demonstrable impact for ongoing, all-inclusive learning is now of public domain. Enhanced productivity and decent working conditions can now materialise in organisations of the region. The possibility is no longer theoretical or a mere conceptual plan. It has given credibility to the messages of training institutions to the community of employers and workers.

Concrete realities of the pilot experiences are evidence that the methodology enhances learning in organisations. They show that it can be adapted to the heterogeneous context of Latin American enterprises and yield good results in individual and collective performance. Moreover, it can be applied without the organisations having previously become "first world" enterprises.

The proposal adequately meets the requirements of international quality standards regarding personnel capabilities, involvement and participation by workers, effectiveness of training activities, enhancement of working conditions and constant improvement processes. It also meets international demands in connection with social responsibility, that in some sectors (the garment industry, for example) have become an important value for end consumers, and that the ILO has been defending through the principles and philosophy of decent work.

The methodology has lived through changes of environment (change of company owners, new political administration) which is an indicator of its soundness. Nevertheless, in all cases there have been high and low peaks, which seems to be a characteristic of the application process. Many organisations are not culturally ready to recognise the importance of informal learning, and facing the slightest difficulty revert to traditional training schemes. Neither are they prepared for working on medium and long term projects, particularly in a context of sudden change. In order to respond to fluctuations that are bound to happen but cannot be foreseen, TVET institutions will have to resort to dynamic planning.

Application of the methodology has shown that the concept of institutional learning does not necessarily coincide with the pathway followed by a TVET institute. In the Dominican case, they both went hand in hand in the initial and expansion stages of the experience. In Mexico, however, the relation between the two has been less close. TVET institutions intervened peripherally, and institutional learning occurred through the participating enterprises, that have externalised their experiences and established informal networks of exchange and learning (to a great extent self-financed).

Significant institutional learning took place in application pathways both in Mexico and the Dominican Republic, a learning that can no doubt be transferred to other contexts. It was shown that it was valid to start at micro level in order to adapt the proposal to the context of a sector and to a country. After advantages and impacts have become evident at micro level, application can be extended. In both cases there was significant acceleration after relevant procedures and routines became established. However, acceleration has limits because the methodology implies changes in the work culture and is necessarily a slow process.

The institutional learning curve has reached a point where it is possible to solve the difficulties that appear when applying the methodology in a controlled context. The challenge is to extend it to uncontrolled situations. There are proposals for replicating the methodology through networks of consultants within and without organisations. However, there have not been concrete experiences in that direction yet.

Employment is an outstanding issue that will have to be incorporated into the process of multiplying the methodology. It is difficult, but not impossible, to consider the objective at micro level within organisations, although sometimes it is opposed to the productivity they seek (which is in turn necessary to maintain employment levels). It is more feasible to consider the generation and conservation of employment at the level of sectors or regions, possibly using adaptations of the training instruments created in organisations.

Getting ahead in that direction and simultaneously consolidating initial experiences is the essence of our agenda for the immediate future. This cannot be divorced from adapting the operation of TVET institutions to the rationale of ongoing, all-inclusive learning in organisations, which is another outstanding issue on the agenda. Cinterfor/ILO can play an important role in the development and implementation of this agenda, being a focal point for the network of institutions involved in institutional learning about continuous, all-inclusive learning in Latin America´s organisations.

BIBLIOGRAPHY

Brown, J.S.; Duguid, P. 2000 *Organizational learning and community-of-practice: to-ward a unified view of working, learning and innovation.* In: Cross, R.; Israelit, S. Strategic learning in a knowledge economy. Woburn: Butterworth-Heinemann.

Cinterfor/OIT. 2000. Boletín técnico interamericano de formación profesional: *Competencias laborales en la formación profesional.* Montevideo. n.149.

—. 2001. Boletín técnico interamericano de formación profesional: *Competencia laboral y valoración del aprendizaje.* Montevideo. n.152

—. 2001 *Formación para el trabajo decente.* Montevideo.

—. 2002. Boletín técnico interamericano de formación profesional: *Formación profesional, productividad y trabajo decente.* Montevideo. n.153.

Cohendet, P.; Llerena, P. 1997 *Learning, technical change, and public policy: how to create and exploit diversity.* In: Edquist, CH. *Systems of innovation.* London: Pinter.

Coutu, D. 2002 *Edgar H. Schein: The anxiety of learning.* Harvard Business Review. Boston.

Cross, R.; Israelit, S. 2000 *Introduction: strategic learning in a knowledge economy: individual, collective and organizational learning process.* In: Cross, R.; Israelit, S. Strategic learning in a knowledge economy. Woburn: Butterworth-Heinemann.

Del Bueno, D. J. 2001 *Buyer beware: The cost of competence.* Nursing Economics. Nov.-Dec.

Eraut, M. y otros. 1997 *The impact of the manager on learning in the workplace: report.* York: Bera.

Festa, P. 2000 *E-learning – transforming the teaching of soft skills.* London, IRS. Competency. Summer.

Galunic, Ch.; Weeks, J. 2001 *A cultural evolution in business thinking.* Financial Times. London. 29th October.

Garrick, J. 2000 *Flexible learning, work and the management of 'intellectual' capital.* In: Jakupec, V.; Garrick, J. Flexible learning, human resource and organisational development . London: Routledge.

Haughey, M. 2000 *A global society needs flexible learning.* In: Jakupec, V.; Garrick, J. Flexible learning, human resource and organisational development. London: Routledge.

INFOTEP. 2001 *Impacto de la metodología de medición y mejoramiento de la productividad en las empresas de República Dominicana.* Santo Domingo.

—. 2001 *Manual de metodología, medición y mejoramiento de la productividad.* Santo Domingo.

Johnson, B. 1992 *Institutional learning.* In: Lundvall, B. *National systems of innovation.* London: Pinter.

Kolb, D. 2000 *The process of experimental learning.* In: Cross, R.; Israelit, S. Strategic learning in a knowledge economy. Woburn: Butterworth-Heinemann.

Labarca, G. (Coord.) 1999 *Formación y empresa: el entrenamiento y la capacitación en el proceso de reestructuración productiva.* Montevideo: Cinterfor/OIT.

—. 2001 *Formación para el trabajo ¿pública o privada?* Montevideo: Cinterfor/OIT.

Langlois, R.; Robertson, P. 1995 *Firms, markets and economic change.* London: Routledge.

Latham, G. 2001 *A missing link in the strategic plan value for money from training can only come about if companies can improve understanding of their strategy and ensure employees can carry it out.* London. Financial Times. 12th November.

Marsh, P. 2001 *A new millennium's winners and losers.* London. Financial Times. 29th October.

Mertens, L. 1996. Competencia laboral: sistemas, surgimiento y modelos. Montevideo: Cinterfor/OIT.

—. 1997 *DACUM (desarrollo de un currículum) y sus variantes SCID y AMOD.* (http://www.leonardmertens.com)

—. 1997 *México: estrategias de mejora de productividad y de recursos humanos en las industrias de alimentos y metalmecánicas.* Lima: OIT.

—. 1997 *La transferibilidad de las nuevas competencias en empresas innovadoras.* México: CONOCER/OIT.

—. 2000 *Dacum- Amod y análisis funcional: una vinculación metodológica.* (http://www.leonardmertens.com)

—. 2000 *La descentralización y el sector privado en la trayectoria de la formación profesional en México.* In: Labarca, G. Formación para el trabajo: ¿pública o privada?. Montevideo: Cinterfor/OIT.

—. 2000 *ISO 9000 y competencia laboral.* (http://www.leonardmertens.com)

Mertens, L.; Wilde, R. 2001 *Aprendizaje organizacional y competencia laboral: la experiencia de un grupo de ingenios azucareros en México.* Santiago de Chile: CEPAL.

Novick, M.; Gallart, M:A: (Coord.) 1997 Competitividad, redes productivas y competencias laborales: ¿homogeneidad o segmentación? Montevideo: Cinterfor/OIT.

Parker, G.; O'Hara, M. 2001 *Developing competencies to recruit disability advisers in Employment Service North West Region.* London. Competency. Autumm.

Pritchard, R. 1990 *Measuring and improving organizational productivity.* New York: Praeger.

Rainbird, H. 2000 *Training in the workplace and workplace training: introduction.* In: Rainbird, H. Training in the workplace. London: Macmillan Press.

Rankin, N. 2001 *Raising performance through people: the eighth competency survey.* London, IRS. Competency. January.

Rodgers, G. 2002 El trabajo decente como una meta para la economía global. *Boletín técnico interamericano de formación profesional: formación profesional, productividad y trabajo decente.* Montevideo, Cinterfor/OIT. n.153.

Rojas, E. 1999 *El saber obrero y la innovación en la empresa: las competencias y las calificaciones laborales.* Montevideo: Cinterfor/OIT.

Román, M.; Díez, E. 1999 *Aprendizaje y currículum.* Madrid: EOS.

Ronco, E.; Lladó, E. 2000 *Aprender a gestionar el cambio.* Barcelona: Paidós.

Ruffier, J. 1998 *La eficiencia productiva: cómo funcionan las fábricas.* Montevideo: Cinterfor/OIT.

Scharmer, C.O. 2001. *Self-transcending knowlegde: organizing around emerging realities.* In: Nonaka, I.; Teece, D. Managing industrial knowledge. London: Sage.

Schoenberger, E. 1997 *The cultural crisis of the firm.* Oxford: Blackwell.

Schulz, M. 2001 *The uncertain relevance of newness: Organizational learning and knowledge flows*. Academy of Management Journal. August.

Schumpeter, J. 1997 *Teoría del desenvolvimiento económico*. México: Fondo de Cultura Económica.

Sengers, L.; Smit, A. 2000 *Iedereen is creatief*. Amsterdam, VNU. Intermediair. 13th July.

Sobek, K.D.; Liker, J.K.; Ward, A.C. 1998 *Another look at how Toyota integrates product development*. Boston. Harvard Business Review. Jul.-Aug.

Spear, S.; Bowen, K. 1999 *Decoding the DNA of the Toyota production system*. Boston. Harvard Business Review. sept.- oct.

Thor, C.G. 1993 *Industry benchmarking*. In: Christopher, W.F. y otros. Handbook for productivity measurement and improvement. Portland: Productivity.

Tolentino, A. 2000 *Labour management cooperation for productivity and competitiveness*. Geneva: ILO.

OIT. 2001 *ILO's productivity forum: Main findings*. Geneva: ILO.

—. 2001 *Reducing the decent work deficit*. Geneva: ILO.

Usher, R. 2000 *Flexible learning, postmodernity and the contemporary workplace*. In: Jakupec, V.; Garrick, J. Flexible learning, human resource and organisational development. London: Routledge.

Warner, J. 2001 *Knowledge management: unlocking potential*. London, IRS. Competency. Spring.

Weggeman, M. 1997 *Kennismanagement*. Scriptium, Schiedam.

Wenger, C.; Snyder, W. 2000 *Communities of practice: The organizational frontier*. Boston. Harvard Business Review. Jan.-Feb.

300.04.2004

Este libro
se terminó de imprimir en el
Departamento de Publicaciones de Cinterfor/OIT
en Montevideo, abril de 2004

Hecho el depósito legal número 330.699/2004

* 9 7 8 9 2 9 0 8 8 1 6 3 6 *